Introduction
to Marxism

Emile Burns

Lawrence & Wishart Ltd
London

First published in 1939 as   MARXISM?
New edition published by   Wishart 1952
New and revised edition 1957
Reprinted 1961
New and revised edition 1966
Reprinted 1971
Reprinted 1974
Reprinted 1976
Reprinted 1978
Reprinted 1983

© Lawrence & Wishart

Photoset in North Wales by
Derek Doyle & Associates, Mold, Clwyd
Printed in Great Britain by
Camelot Press, Southampton

CONTENTS

Chapter 1

A Scientific View of the World

Marxism is a general theory of the world in which we live, and of human society as a part of that world. It takes its name from Karl Marx (1818-1883), who, together with Friedrich Engels (1820-1895), worked out the theory during the middle and latter part of last century.

They set out to discover why human society is what it is, why it changes, and what further changes are in store for mankind. Their studies led them to the conclusion that these changes – like the changes in external nature – are not accidental, but follow certain laws. This fact makes it possible to work out a *scientific* theory of society, based on the actual experience of men, as opposed to the vague notions about society which used to be (and still are) put forward – notions associated with religious beliefs, race and hero-worship, personal inclinations or utopian dreams.

Marx applied this general idea to the society in which he lived – mainly capitalist Britain – and worked out the economic theory of capitalism by which he is most widely known. But he always insisted that his economic theories could not be separated from his historical and social theories. Profits and wages can be studied up to a certain point as purely economic problems; but the student who sets out to study real life and not abstractions soon realises that profits and wages can only be fully understood when *employers and workers* are brought into the picture; and these in turn lead on to a study of the *historical stage* in which they live.

The scientific approach to the development of society is based, like all science, on experience, on the facts of history and of the world round us. Therefore Marxism is not a completed, finished theory. As history unfolds, as man gathers more experience, Marxism is constantly being developed and applied to the new facts that have come to light.

The result of the scientific approach to the study of society is knowledge that can be used to change society, just as all scientific knowledge can be used to change the external world. But it also makes clear that the general laws which govern the movement of society are of the same pattern as the laws of the external world. These laws which hold good universally, both for men and things, make up what may be called the Marxist philosophy or view of the world.

The following chapters deal with Marxist theory in the fields which are of most immediate interest. It is essential, however, for the student to realise from the outset that Marxism claims recognition because it is drawn from a scientific study of the facts; because its theories correspond with the facts; in a word, because it is true. And because it is true, it can be and should be used to rid humanity for ever of the evils and misery which afflict so many in the world today, and to help men and women forward to full development in a higher form of society.

Chapter 2

The Laws of Social Development

The history of mankind is often presented in the form of a record of wars between nations and the exploits of individual monarchs, generals or statesmen. Sometimes the motives of these individuals are described in a purely personal way – their ambitions led them to conquer territory, or their moral or immoral outlook caused them to adopt certain policies. Sometimes they are described as acting for the sake of the country's honour or prestige, or from some motive of religion.

Marxism is not satisfied with such an approach to history.

In the first place, it considers that the real science of history must deal with the peoples. It regards Cromwell, who led the English revolution of 1640, as important because he and his movement broke down the barriers of feudalism, and opened the way for the widespread development of capitalism in Britain. What matters is not the record of his battles and his religious outlook and intrigues. But the study of Cromwell's place in the development of British production and distribution, the understanding of why, at that period and in Britain, the struggle developed against the feudal monarchy; the study of the changes actually brought about in that period – these are important; they are the basis of a *science* of history. By using the knowledge derived from such a study (along with the study of other periods and of other peoples), it is possible to draw up general theories – *laws* of the development of society, which are just as real as the laws of chemistry or any other science. And once we know these laws we can make use of them, just as we can make use of any scientific law – we can not only foretell what is likely to happen, but can *act* in such a way as to make sure that it does happen.

So Marxism approaches the study of history in order to trace the natural laws which run through all human history, and for this purpose it looks not at individuals but at peoples. And when it looks at peoples (after the stage of primitive society) it finds that there are different sections of the people, some pulling one way and some another, not as individuals, but as *classes*.

What are these classes? In the simplest terms, they are sections of the people who get their living in the same way. In feudal society the monarch and the feudal lords got their living from some form of tribute (whether personal service or payments in kind) taken from their "serfs," who actually produced things, mainly on the land. The feudal lords were a class, with interests as a class – they all wanted to get as much as possible out of the labour of their serfs; they all wanted to extend their land and the number of serfs working for them. On the other hand, the serfs were a class, with their own class interests. They wanted to keep more of what they produced for themselves and their families, instead of handing it over to their lords; they wanted freedom to work for themselves; they wanted to do away with the harsh treatment they received at the hands of their lords, who were also their law-makers and their judges.

Hence in every feudal country there was a constant struggle going on between the lords and the serfs, sometimes only on an individual basis, or a group of serfs against their particular lord; sometimes on a much wider basis, when large numbers of serfs acted together, in order to try to get their general conditions of life made easier. The revolt of 1381 in England, led by John Ball and Wat Tyler, is an instance of this. Similar risings of serfs or peasants occurred in Germany, Russia and many other countries, while the struggle was continually going on on a smaller scale.

In addition to the obligations to work their lord's land, there were many forms of tribute to be paid in kind – not only a share of the produce of their own holding, but products of the handicraft of the serfs and their families. There were some specialised producers – for example, makers of weapons and equipment. And there were merchants who bought surplus products, trading them for the products of other regions or countries. With the increase of trade, these merchants began to need more than the surplus produced by serfs and not required by their lords; they therefore began to develop organised production for the market, providing the serfs or peasants with raw materials and buying what they produced. Some of the freed serfs also managed to set themselves up in the towns as free craftsmen, producing cloth, metalware and other articles. So in a slow development, lasting hundreds of years, there grew up within feudal production for local consumption, also production for the market, carried on by independent artisans and employers of wage-labour. The independent artisans also gradually developed into *employers of labour*, with "journeymen" working for them for wages. So from the sixteenth century onwards there was coming into existence a new class, the industrial capitalist class, with its shadow", the industrial working class. In the countryside, too, the old feudal obligations had broken down – personal service was changed into money rent, the serfs were transformed in many cases into free peasants each on his holding, and the landowner began to pay wages for the labour-power he needed on his own farms; in this way, too, the capitalist farmer came into existence, along with the farm labourer earning wages.

But the growth of the capitalist class in town and country did not automatically put an end to the former ruling class of feudal lords. On the contrary, the monarchy, the old landed aristocracy and the Church did their utmost to use the new capitalism for their own benefit. The serfs who had been freed or escaped to the towns had also escaped from having to pay tribute (in personal service, in kind or in money) to the lords. But when the descendants of these serfs grew relatively rich, they began to find that they were not really free – the king and the feudal nobility made them pay taxes of all kinds, imposed restrictions on their trade, and prevented the free development of their manufacturing business.

The king and the old landed nobility were able to do this because they controlled the machinery of the State – armed forces, judges and prisons; while they also made the laws. Therefore the growth of the capitalist class also meant the growth of new forms of class struggle. The capitalists had to engage in a struggle against the monarchy and the feudal lords, a struggle which continued over several centuries. In some relatively backward countries it is still going on – but in Britain and France, for example, it has been completed.

How did this come about?

In Britain, where this stage was reached far earlier than in other countries, the struggle of the growing capitalist class against taxation and restrictions reached a high point in the middle of the seventeenth century. These restrictions were holding back the expansion of the capitalist form of production. The capitalists tried to get them removed by peaceful means – by petitions to the king, by refusing to pay taxes, and so on; but nothing far-reaching could be won against the machinery of the State. Therefore the capitalists had to meet force with force; they had to rouse the people against the king, against arbitrary taxation and trade restrictions, against the arrests and penalties imposed by the king's judges for all attempts to break through the feudal barriers. In other words, the capitalists had to organise an armed revolution, to lead the people to rise in arms against the king and the old forms of oppression – to defeat the former rulers by military means. Only after this had been done was it possible for the capitalist class to become the ruling class, to break down all barriers to the development of capitalism, and to make the laws needed for this.

It is perfectly true that this capitalist revolution in England is presented as a fight against Charles I because he was a despotic, scheming monarch of Roman Catholic leanings, while Cromwell is represented as a highly respectable anti-Catholic, with great ideals of British freedom. The struggle, in short, is presented as a moral, religious fight. Marxism goes deeper than the individuals, and deeper than the watchwords under which the fight was carried on. It sees the essence of the struggle of that period as the fight of the rising capitalist class to take power from the old feudal ruling class. And in fact it was a clear turning-point: after that revolution, and the second stage of it in 1688, the capitalist class won an increasing share in the control of the State.

In England, owing to the early stage at which the capitalist revolution came, the victory of the capitalists was not decisive and not complete. As a result of this, though the old feudal relations were largely destroyed, the landowning class (including rich recruits from the towns) to a great extent survived, merging with the moneyed interests over the next two centuries, and keeping a considerable share in the control of the State.

But in France, where the whole process came later, and the capitalist revolution did not take place until 1789, the immediate changes were more far-reaching. To the Marxist, however, this was not due to the fact that Rousseau and other writers had written works proclaiming the rights of man, nor to the fact that the popular watchwords of the revolution were "Liberty – Equality – Fraternity." Just as the essence of the Cromwell revolution is to be found in the class struggle and not in the religious watchwords, so the essence of the

French revolution is to be found in the class relations and not in the abstract principles of justice inscribed on its banners.

Marx says of such periods: "Just as we cannot judge an individual on the basis of his own opinion of himself, so such a revolutionary period cannot be judged from its own consciousness." (Introduction to *The Critique of Political Economy*). What is important for the understanding of revolutionary periods is to see the classes struggling for power, the new class taking power from the old; even if, consciously or unconsciously, the leaders of the new class proclaim their fight to be for what are apparently abstract ideas or issues not directly connected with the questions of class interests and class power.

The Marxist approach to history sees the struggle between contending classes as the principal driving force in the development of human society. But the division of society into classes, and the rise of new classes, depends on the stage of development of the productive forces used by man to produce the things he needs for life. The discovery of power-driven machinery was an immense step forward in production; but it was not only this. It also brought with it the destruction of the producer owning his own spinning-wheel and weaving-frame, who could no longer compete against rival producers using power-driven machinery which enabled a worker to spin and weave in one day more than the artisan could produce in a week. Therefore the individual producer, who owned and used his own instruments of production, gave place to two groups of people – the capitalist class, who owned the new power-driven machinery but did not work it; and the industrial working class, which did not own any means of production, but worked (for wages) for the owner.

This change came about unconsciously, without being planned by anyone; it was the direct result of the new knowledge gained by a few people who applied it to production for their own advantage, but without in any way foreseeing or desiring the social consequences that followed from it. Marx held that this was true of all previous changes in human society: man was steadily increasing his knowledge, applying his new-found knowledge to production, and by this causing profound social changes. These social changes led to class conflicts, which took the form of conflicts over ideas or institutions – religion, parliament, justice and so on – because the ideas and institutions then current had grown up on the basis of the old mode of production and the old class relations. —

What brought such ideas and institutions into existence and what brought them to an end? Marx pointed out that always and everywhere the ideas and institutions only grew up out of the actual practice of men. The first thing was: the production of the means of life – of food and clothing and shelter. In every historical social group – the primitive tribe, slave society, feudal society, modern capitalist society – the relations between the members of the group depended on the form of production. Institutions were not thought out in advance, but grew up out of what was customary in each group; institutions, laws, moral precepts and other ideas merely crystallised, as it were, out of customs, and the customs were directly associated with the form of production.

It follows, therefore, that when the form of production changed – for example from feudalism to capitalism – the institutions and ideas also changed. What was moral at one stage could become immoral at another, and *vice versa*. And naturally at the time when the material change was taking place – the change in the form of production – there was always a conflict of ideas, a challenge to existing institutions.

With the actual growth of capitalist production and its

conflict with feudalism there came up conflicting ideas: not divine right, but "no taxation without representation," the right to trade freely, and new religious conceptions expressing more individual right, less centralised control. But what seemed to be free men fighting to the death for abstract rights and religious forms was in fact the struggle between rising capitalism and dying feudalism; the conflict of *ideas* was secondary.

Marxists do not set up abstract "principles" for the organisation of society. Marxism considers that all such "principles" as have appeared in human thought merely reflect the actual organisation of society at a particular time and place, and do not and cannot hold good always and everywhere. Moreover, ideas that seem to be universal – such as the idea of human equality – in fact do not mean the same thing in different stages of society. In the Greek city States, the idea of the equal rights of men did not apply to slaves; the "liberty, equality and fraternity" of the great French Revolution meant the liberty of the rising capitalist class to trade freely, the equality of this class with the feudal lords, and the fraternity of this class with itself – the mutual aid against feudal oppressions and restrictions. None of these ideas applied to the slaves in the French colonies, or even to the poorer sections of the population in France itself.

Hence we can say that ideas connected with the organisation of society are, as a rule, *class* ideas, the ideas of the dominant class in society, which imposes them on the rest of society through its ownership of the machinery of propaganda, its control of education and its power to punish contrary ideas through the law courts, through dismissals and similar measures. This does not mean that the dominant class says to itself: Here is an idea which of course isn't true, but we will force other people to believe it, or at least not to deny it in public. On the contrary, the dominant class does not as a rule invent such ideas. The ideas come up out of actual life – the actual power of the feudal lord or of the rich industrialist who has been created a peer is the material basis for the idea that "noblemen" are superior to other people. But once the idea has come up and been established, it becomes important for the dominant class to make sure that everyone accepts it – for if people do not accept it, this means that they will challenge the king's divine right (and perhaps even go to the length of cutting off his head). So the dominant class of any period and any country – not only the United States – does what it can to prevent "dangerous thoughts" from spreading.

But, it may be asked, if ideas are secondary, if the primary fact is always the material change in the form of production, how can any "dangerous thoughts" arise? How, in short, can people think of a new form of production before it actually arises?

The answer is that they cannot think of it before the conditions for its existence have appeared. But they are *made* to think of it when these conditions have appeared, by the very conflict between the old conditions and the new forces of production.

For example, with the actual growth of production by wage-labour, and the necessity to sell the products in order to realise the profit, the early capitalist was brought up sharply against the feudal restrictions on trade. Hence the idea of freedom from restrictions, of having a say in fixing taxes, and so on. It was not yet capitalist society, but the conditions for a capitalist society had arisen, and out of these came the capitalist ideas.

But although ideas can only arise from material conditions, when they do arise they certainly exert an influence on men's actions and therefore on the course of things. Ideas based on the old system of production are conservative – they hold back men's actions, and that is why the dominant class in each period does everything it can to teach these ideas. But ideas based on the new conditions of production are progressive – they encourage action to carry through the change to the new system, and that is why the dominant class regards them as dangerous. Thus the idea that a social system is bad which destroys food to keep up prices, at a time when large numbers of people are in a state of semi-starvation, is clearly a "dangerous thought." It leads on to the idea of a system in which production is for use and not for profit; and this leads to the organisation of socialist and communist parties, which begin to work to bring about the change to the new system.

The Marxist conception of social development (known as "historical materialism") is therefore not a materialist "determinism" – the theory that man's actions are absolutely determined by the material world round him. On the contrary, man's actions, and the material changes which these actions bring about, are the product partly of the material world outside him, and partly of his own knowledge of how to control the material world. But he only gets this knowledge through experience of the material world, which, so to speak, comes first. He gets the experience of the material world not in an abstract, arm-chair way, but in the course of producing the things he needs for life. And as his knowledge increases, as he invents new methods of production and operates them, the old forms of social organisation become a barrier, preventing the full use of the new methods. The exploited class becomes aware of this from the actual practice of life; it fights first against particular evils, particular barriers created by the old form of social organisation. But inevitably it is drawn into a *general fight* against the ruling class in order to change the system.

Up to a certain point, the whole process by which new productive forces develop out of the old system is unconscious and unplanned, and so also is the struggle against the old forms of social organisation which preserve the old system. But always a stage is reached when the old class relations are seen to be the barrier preventing the new productive forces from being fully used; it is at this stage that the conscious action of "the class with the future in its hands" comes into play.

But the process of developing the productive forces need no longer be unconscious and unplanned. Man has accumulated sufficient experience, sufficient knowledge of the laws of social change, to pass on to the next stage in a conscious and planned way, and to set up a society in which production is conscious and planned. Engels says of that stage:

"The objective, external forces which have hitherto dominated history will then pass under the control of men themselves. It is only from this point that men, with full consciousness, will fashion their own history."

Chapter 3

Capitalist Society

A great part of Marx's life was devoted to the study of capitalism – the method of production which had succeeded feudalism in Britain and was establishing itself all over the world in the course of last century. The aim of his study was to discover the "law of motion" of capitalist society. Capitalism had not always existed, but had grown up gradually; it was not the same in Marx's day as it had been at the time of the "industrial revolution" in Britain in the latter part of the eighteenth century. The problem was not merely to describe the capitalist method of production of his own time, but to make an analysis which would show why and in what direction it was changing. This approach to the question was new. Other writers on economic matters took capitalism as it was, and described it as if it was a fixed, eternal system; for Marx, this method of production, like all others in history, was changing. The result of his study was therefore not only a description, but a scientific forecast, because he was able to see the way in which capitalism was in fact developing.

The feudal form of production gradually gave way to production for profit, which is the essential mark of capitalism. Production for profit required two things: someone with enough resources to buy means of production (looms, spinning-machines and so on); and, secondly, people who had no means of production themselves, no resources by using which they could live. In other words, there had to be "capitalists," who owned means of production, and workers whose only chance of getting a livelihood was to work the machines owned by the capitalists.

The workers produced things, not directly for themselves or for the personal use of their new "lord," the capitalist, but for the capitalist to sell for money. Things made in this way are called "commodities" – that is, articles produced for sale on the market. The worker received wages, the employer received profit – something that was left after the customer had paid for the articles, and after the capitalist had paid wages, the cost of raw materials and other costs of production.

What was the source of this profit? Marx pointed out that it could not possibly come from the capitalists selling the products above their value – this would mean that all capitalists were all the time cheating each other, and where one made a "profit" of this kind the other necessarily made a loss, and the profits and losses would cancel each other, leaving no general profit. It therefore followed that the value of an article on the market must already contain the profit: the profit must arise in the course of production, and not in the sale of the product.

The enquiry must therefore lead to an examination of the process of production, to see whether there is some factor in production which adds value greater than its cost (its own value).

But first it is necessary to ask what is meant by "value." In ordinary language, value can have two quite distinct meanings. It may mean value for use by someone – a thirsty man "values" a drink; a particular thing may have a "sentimental value" for someone. But there is also another meaning in ordinary use – the value of a thing when sold on the market, by any seller to any buyer, which is what is known as its "exchange value."

Now it is true that, even in a capitalist system, particular things may be produced for particular buyers and a special price arranged; but what Marx was concerned with was normal capitalist production – the system under which millions of tons of products of all kinds are being produced for the market in general, for any buyer that can be found. What gives products their normal "exchange value" on the market? Why, for example, has a yard of cloth more exchange value than a pin?

Exchange value is measured in terms of money; an article is "worth" a certain amount of money. But what makes it possible for things to be compared with each other in value, whether through money or for direct exchange? Marx pointed out that things can only be compared in this way if there is something common to all of them, of which some have more and some less, so that a comparison is possible. This common factor is obviously not weight or colour or any other physical property; nor is it "use value" for human life (necessary foods have far less exchange value than motor cars) or any other abstraction. There is only one factor common to all products – they are produced by human labour. A thing has greater exchange value if more human labour has been put into its production; exchange value is determined by the "labour-time" spent on each article.

But, of course, not the individual labour-time. When things are bought and sold on a general market, their exchange value as individual products is averaged out, and the exchange value of any particular yard of cloth of a certain weight and quality is determined by the "average socially necessary labour-time" required for its production.

If this is the general basis for the exchange value of things produced under capitalism, what determines the amount of wages paid to the actual producer, the worker? Marx put the question in precisely the same way: what is the common factor between things produced under capitalism and labour-power under capitalism, which we know also has an exchange value on the market? There is no such factor other than the factor which we have already seen determines the exchange value of ordinary products – the labour-time spent in producing them. What is meant by the labour-time spent in producing labour-power? It is the time (the average "socially necessary" time) spent in producing the food, shelter, warmth and other things which keep the worker going from week to week. In normal capitalist society, the things necessary to maintain the family of the worker have also to be taken into account. The labour-time necessary for producing all these things determines the exchange value of the worker's labour-power, which he sells to the capitalist for wages.

But while, in modern capitalist society, the time spent in maintaining the worker's labour-power may be only four hours a day, his power to labour lasts eight, ten or more hours a day. For the first four hours each day, therefore, his actual labour is producing the equivalent of what is paid to him in wages; for the remaining hours of his working day he is producing "surplus value" which his employer appropriates. This is the source of capitalist profit – the value produced by the worker over and above the value of his own keep – that is, the wages he receives.

This brief statement of Marx's analysis of value and surplus value needs to be made more exact in many ways, and there is not space to cover every variation. But a few of the general points can be indicated.

The term "exchange value" has been used, because this is the basis of the whole analysis. But in actual life things hardly ever sell at precisely their exchange value. Whether material products or human labour power, they are bought and sold on the market at a *price*, which may be either above or below the correct exchange value. There may be a surplus of the particular product on the market, and the price that day may be far below the correct exchange value; or, if there is a shortage, the price may rise above the value. These fluctuations in price are, in fact, influenced by "supply and demand," and this led many capitalist economists to think that supply and demand was the sole factor in price. But it is clear that supply and demand only cause fluctuations about a definite level. What that level is, whether it is one penny or a hundred pounds, is clearly not determined by supply and demand, but by the labour-time used in producing the article.

The actual price of labour-power – the actual wages paid – is also influenced by supply and demand; but it is influenced by other factors as well – the strength of trade union organisation in particular. Nevertheless, the price of labour-power in ordinary capitalist society always fluctuates around a definite level – the equivalent of the worker's keep, taking into account that the various grades and groups of workers have varying needs, which are themselves largely the result of previous trade union struggles establishing a standard above the lowest minimum standard for existence.

The labour-power of different grades of workers is not, of course, identical in value; an hour's work of a skilled engineer produces more value than an hour's work of an unskilled labourer. Marx showed that such differences were in fact accounted for when articles were sold on the market, which, as he put it, recorded a definite relation between what the more skilled worker made in an hour and what the labourer made in an hour.

How does this difference in value come about? Marx answers: not on any "principle" that skill is ethically better than lack of skill or any other abstract notion. The fact that a skilled worker's labour-power has more exchange value than the labourer's is due to exactly the same factor that makes a steamship more valuable than a rowing boat – more human labour has gone to the making of it. The whole process of training the skilled worker, besides the higher standard of living which is essential for the maintenance of his skill, involves more labour-time.

Another point to note is that if the intensity of labour is

increased beyond what was the previous average, this is equivalent to a longer labour-time; eight hours of intensified labour may produce values equivalent to ten or twelve hours of what was previously normal labour.

What is the importance of the analysis made by Marx to show the source of profit? It is that it explains the class struggle of the capitalist period. In each factory or other enterprise the wages paid to the workers are not the equivalent of the full value they produce, but only equal to about half this value, or even less. The rest of the value produced by the worker during his working day (i.e. after he has produced the equivalent of his wages) is taken outright by his employer. The employer is therefore constantly trying to increase the amount taken from the worker. He can do this in several ways: for example, by reducing the worker's wages; this means that the worker works a lesser proportion of the day for himself, and a greater proportion for the employer. The same result is achieved by "speeding up" or intensifying the labour – the worker produces his keep in a smaller proportion of the working day, and works a larger proportion for his employer. The same result, again, is achieved by lengthening the working day, which increases the proportion of the working day spent in working for the employer. On the other hand, the worker fights to improve his own position by demanding higher wages and shorter hours and by resisting "speeding up."

Hence the continuous struggle between the capitalists and the workers, which can never end so long as the capitalist system of production lasts. This struggle, starting on the basis of the individual worker or group of workers fighting an individual employer, gradually widens out. Trade union organisation on the one hand, and employers' organisation on the other, bring great sections of each class into action against each other. Finally, political organisations of the workers are built up, which as they extend can bring all industrial groups and other sections of the people into action against the capitalist class. In its highest form, this struggle becomes revolution – the overthrow of the capitalist class and the establishment of a new system of production in which the workers do not work part of the day for the benefit of another class. This point is worked out more fully in later chapters; the essential thing to note is that the class struggle under capitalism is due to the character of capitalist production itself – the antagonistic interests of the two classes, which continually clash in the process of production.

Having analysed wages and profits, we now pass to the study of capital. First it must be noted that the "surplus value" created by the worker in the course of production is not all kept by his employer. It is, so to speak, a fund from which different capitalist groups take their pickings – the landowner takes rent, the banker takes interest, the middleman takes his "merchant's profit," and the actual industrial employer only gets what is left as his own profit. This in no way affects the preceding analysis; it only means that all these capitalist sections are, as it were, carrying on a certain subsidiary struggle among themselves for the division of the spoils. But they are all united in wanting to get the utmost possible out of the working class.

What is capital?

It has many physical forms: machinery, buildings, raw materials, fuel and other things required for production; it is also money used to pay wages for production.

Yet not all machinery, buildings and so on, and not even all sums of money are capital. For example, a peasant on the west coast of Ireland may have some sort of building to live in, with a few yards of ground round it; he may have some livestock, and a boat of some sort; he may even have some little sum of money. But if he is his own master and nobody else's master, none of his property is capital.

Property (whatever the physical form) only becomes capital in the economic sense when it is used to produce surplus value; that is, when it is used to employ workers, who in the course of producing things also produce surplus value.

What is the origin of such capital?

Looking back through history, the early accumulation of capital was very largely open robbery. Vast quantities of capital in the form of gold and other costly things were looted by adventurers, from America, India and Africa. But this was not the only way in which capital came into being through robbery. In Britain itself, the whole series of "Enclosure Acts" stole the common lands for the benefit of the capitalist farmers. And in doing so, they deprived the peasantry of their means of living, and thus turned them into proletarians – workers with no possibility of living except by working the land taken from them for the benefit of the new owner, or by finding some other capitalist employer. Marx shows that this is the real origin of capital ("primitive accumulation"), and he ridicules the legend that capitalists were originally abstemious men who "saved" from their meagre living:

"This primitive accumulation plays in Political Economy about the same part as original sin in theology ... In times long gone by there were two sorts of people; one the diligent, intelligent and, above all, frugal elite; the other, lazy rascals, spending their substance, and more, in riotous living ... Thus it came to pass that the former sort accumulated wealth, and the latter sort had at last nothing to sell except their own skins. And from this original sin dates the poverty of the great majority, that, despite all its labour, has up to now nothing to sell but itself, and the wealth of the few that increases constantly although they have long ceased to work."

(*Capital*, Vol. I. Ch. XXVI).

But capital does not remain at the level of primitive accumulation; it has increased at an enormous rate. Even if the original capital was the product of direct robbery, what is the source of the additional capital piled up since that period?

Indirect robbery, Marx answers. Making the worker work more hours than is necessary for his keep, and appropriating the value of what he makes in those extra hours of work – the "surplus value." The capitalist uses a part of this surplus value for his own maintenance; the balance is used as *new capital* – that is to say, he adds to it his previous capital, and is thus able to employ more workers and take more surplus value in the next turnover of production, which in turn means more capital – and so on *ad infinitum*.

Or, rather, it would go on to infinity but for the fact that other economic and social laws come into play. In the long run, the most important obstacle is the class struggle, which from time to time hinders the whole process and eventually ends it altogether by ending capitalist production. But there are many other obstacles to the smooth course of capitalist development, which also arise out of the nature of capitalism.

Economic crises occur which check the expansion of capital, and even lead to the destruction of part of the capital accumulated in previous years. "In these crises," Marx says (*Communist Manifesto*, 1848), "there broke out an epidemic that, in all earlier epochs, would have seemed an absurdity – the epidemic of over-production." In feudal society, a bumper wheat harvest would have meant more food for everyone; in capitalist society, it may mean starvation for workers thrown out of employment because the wheat cannot be sold, and therefore less wheat is sown next year.

The features of capitalist crises were only too familiar in the years between the two wars: there is over-production, therefore new production declines and workers are unemployed; their unemployment means a further decline in the market demand, so more factories slow down production; new factories are not put up, and some are even destroyed (shipyards on the north-east coast or cotton spindles and looms in Lancashire); wheat and other products are destroyed, though the unemployed and their families suffer hunger and illness. It is a madman's world; but at last the stocks are used up or destroyed, production begins to increase, trade develops, there is more employment – and there is steady recovery for a year or two, leading to an apparently boundless expansion of production; until suddenly once more there is over-production and crisis, and the whole process begins again.

What is the cause of these crises? Marx answers: it is a law of capitalist production that each block of capital strives to expand – to make more profit, and therefore to produce and sell more products. The more capital, the more production. But at the same time, the more capital, the less labour-power employed: machinery takes the place of men (what we know now as "rationalisation" of industry). In other words, the more capital, the more production and the less wages, therefore the less demand for the products made. (It should perhaps be made clear that it need not be an *absolute* fall in total wages; usually the crisis comes from a *relative* fall, that is, total wages may actually increase in a boom, but they increase *less* than total production, so that demand falls behind output).

This disproportion between the expansion of capital and the relative stagnation of the workers' demand is the ultimate cause of crises. But, of course, the moment at which the crisis becomes apparent, and the particular way it develops, may depend on quite other factors – to take an example from the USA in 1950 onwards, a big armaments production (i.e. a Government "demand" which is right outside the normal capitalist process) may partially conceal for a time the fact that crisis conditions are developing. So may other factors such as the Government buying up of surplus farm products, or a great expansion of consumer credit – instalment buying. But none of these factors alter the growing gap between production and consumption; they merely postpone the crisis.

Then there is another most important factor in the development of capitalism – competition. Like all other factors in capitalist production, it has two contradictory results. On the one hand, because of competition to win larger sales of products, each capitalist enterprise is constantly trying to reduce production costs, especially by saving wages – through direct wage reductions or by speeding-up labour-saving devices, the latest form of which is known as automation. On the other hand, those enterprises which succeed in getting enough capital to improve their technique and produce with less labour are thereby contributing to the reduction of demand owing to the total wages paid out being reduced.

Nevertheless, the enterprise which improves its technique makes a higher rate of profit for a time – until its competitors follow suit and also produce with less labour. But not all its competitors can follow suit. As the average concern gets larger and larger, greater amounts of capital are needed to modernise a plant, and the number of companies that can keep up the pace grows smaller. The other concerns go to the wall – they become bankrupt and are either taken over by their bigger competitors or are closed down altogether. "One capitalist kills many." Thus in each branch of industry the number of separate concerns is steadily reduced: big trusts appear, which more or less dominate a particular field of industry. Thus out of capitalist competition comes its opposite – capitalist monopoly. This brings out new features, which are described in the next chapter.

Chapter 4

The Imperialist Stage of Capitalism

In popular usage, imperialism is a policy of expansion, the conquest of less developed countries to form an Empire. In so far as the policy is seen to be more than an abstract desire to see the country's flag floating over as much territory as possible, it is recognised that there is some economic reason for the policy of expansion. It is sometimes said, for example, that the reason is the need for markets, or for raw materials and food, or for land where an overcrowded home population could find an outlet.

But foreign countries can be perfectly good markets. Raw materials and food supplies can always be obtained from foreign countries. And as for land for settlement, it is only the conditions created by capitalism that drive people out of their own country and force them to seek a living in someone else's country. What then are the causes of imperialist expansion?

The first Marxist analysis of modern imperialism was made by Lenin. He pointed out that one of its special features was the export of capital, as distinct from the export of ordinary commodities; and he showed that this was the result of certain changes that had taken place within capitalism itself. He therefore described imperialism as a special stage of capitalism – the stage in which monopolies on a larger scale had developed in the chief capitalist countries.

In the early days of industrial capitalism the factories, mines and other enterprises were very small. As a rule they were owned by a family group or a small group of partners, who were able to provide the relatively small amount of capital that was required to start up a factory or a mine. Each new technical development, however, made more capital necessary; while, on the other hand, the market for industrial products was constantly expanding – at the expense of handicraft production, first in Britain and then in other countries. The size of industrial enterprises, therefore grew rapidly. With the invention of railways and steamships the iron, and later the steel, industry developed, involving enterprises of much greater size. Whatever the industry, the larger enterprise was more economical to run, and tended to make more profits and expand more rapidly. Many of the smaller enterprises could not compete, and closed down or were absorbed by their more powerful rivals.

Thus a double process was constantly at work: production tended to be more and more concentrated in larger enterprises and the proportion of production controlled by a small number of very rich people was constantly increasing.

Marx was well aware of the process that was taking place even in his day, and called attention to the increasing technical concentration, i.e. the concentration of production in large units, secondly, to the concentration of capital in the ownership or control of a smaller and smaller group of individuals. He saw that the inevitable result would be the replacement of free competition by monopoly, and that this would bring out all the difficulties inherent in capitalism in a more intense form.

By the beginning of this century economic writers (especially J.A. Hobson in Britain) were noting the great degree of monopoly that had already been reached in many industries. In 1916, during the First World War, Lenin (in *Imperialism: the Highest Stage of Capitalism*) brought together the various facts already known about the growth of monopolies, and turned his attention to the political and social as well as the purely economic features of monopoly. On the basis of the developments since Marx's death, he was able to develop and extend the conclusions reached by Marx. Lenin showed that in the imperialist stage of capitalism, which he regarded as having developed by about 1900, there were five economic features to be noted:

(1) The concentration of production and of capital had developed to such an extent that it had created monopolies which played an important part in economic life.

This had taken place in every advanced capitalist country, but particularly in Germany and the United States. The process has, of course, continued at an increasing rate; in Britain such concerns as Imperial Chemical Industries, with net assets of £458 million in 1955, and Unilever, with net assets of £415 million in 1955, are outstanding examples. In every industry a very large proportion of the total trade is done by a few big concerns, which are usually linked together by agreements for price-fixing, quotas and so on, thus in effect exerting a joint monopoly.

(2) Bank capital had merged with industrial capital, creating a "finance-capital" oligarchy which virtually ruled each country.

This point requires some explanation. In the early days the industrial capitalists were distinct from the bankers, who had little or no direct interests in industrial concerns, although, of course, they lent money to them and took a share of the profits in the form of interest. But with the growth of industry and the wide establishment of the "share company," the men who owned the banks also began to take shares in industrial companies, while the richer industrialists took shares in the banks. Thus the very richest capitalists, whether they started as bankers or industrialists, became banker-industrialists.

This combination of capitalist functions in one and the same group enormously increased their power. (In Britain particularly, the big landowners also merged with this group.) The bank, working with an industrial concern with which it was linked in this way, could help that concern by lending it money, by making loans to other companies on condition that orders were placed with the concern in which the bank was interested, and so on. Thus the finance-capital group was able rapidly to increase its wealth and its monopoly control of one section of industry after another; and, needless to say, its voice received greater attention from the State.

The best illustration of the merging of the banks with industry is the increasing number of directorships in other concerns held by the directors of banks. Of course this does not mean that the banks own the other concerns; the point is that the powerful figures in the banking world are also the powerful figures in industry and trade – they form the same group of very rich men whose capital runs through the whole of British capitalism. In 1870 the directors of the banks which later became the "Big Five" and the Bank of England held 157 other directorships; in 1913 they held 329; in 1939 they held 1,150. The full force of these figures is all the greater when it is realised that the 1939 figure includes such concerns as Unilever and I.C.I., which themselves have swallowed large numbers of smaller enterprises.

(3) The export of capital, as distinguished from the export of commodities, grew in importance.

In the earlier period of capitalism, Britain exported textile and other manufactures to other countries, and with the proceeds bought local products, thus in effect exchanging her manufactures for the raw materials and food required for British industry. But in the second half of last century, and particularly at its end, finance capital grew more and more concerned in exporting capital, with a view not to a trade exchange but to drawing interest on this capital from year to year. Such exports of capital – lending to foreign states or companies, or financing railways and harbour works or mines in other countries – were usually made on the condition that orders for materials, etc., were placed with the British industrial concerns with which the banks were connected. Thus the two wings of finance capital worked together, each getting very substantial profits and shutting out rivals.

(4) International monopoly combines of capitalists were formed and divided up the world between them.

This took place in steel, oil and many other industries; it was agreed between the monopoly groups in different countries what share each should have in total foreign trade; often particular markets were allocated to each and fixed prices were agreed. The limits of such agreements are explained later.

(5) The territorial division of the world by the greatest Powers was virtually completed. (The percentage of Africa belonging to European Powers was 11 in 1876, and 90 in 1900.)

The importance of this was that the easy annexation of more or less defenceless countries could no longer continue. The finance-capital groups in the wealthiest States could no longer expand the territories they controlled *except at each other's expense* – that is to say, only by large-scale wars to redivide the world in favour of the victorious state.

One of the special points made by Lenin in this connection is of particular interest. The drive of each imperialist country for expansion had generally been treated as only aimed at colonial countries. Lenin pointed out that this was by no means essential; the drive was general, and in suitable circumstances would be directed against other industrially developed states. The drive of German finance-capital in the Nazi period was a clear example of this.

On the basis of this whole analysis, Lenin drew the conclusion that the imperialist stage of capitalism inevitably brought with it greater economic crises, wars on a world scale and, on the other hand, working-class revolutions and the revolt of oppressed peoples in the colonies and semi-colonial areas against their exploitation by imperialists.

The concentration of capital in the hands of small groups also meant that these groups got more and more power over the State machine, so that the policy of the various countries became more closely associated with the interests of these narrow groups. It is this factor which made it possible for the finance-capital group in each country to fight their foreign rivals by tariffs, quotas and other State measures, and in the last resort by war.

Why is this conflict between rival groups inevitable? Why can they not agree to parcel out the world between themselves?

It was noted above that the monopoly groups in different countries make agreements to divide the markets of the world between them. In the abstract, this might seem to lead to the complete elimination of competition, and to a kind of international merging of interests of a permanent character. But Lenin brought forward facts to show that such international agreements were never lasting. An agreement made in 1905 would be on the basis of allocating the markets in relation to the producing powers at that time of the different groups, say British, French, German and American. Unequal development, however, is a law of the growth of capital. Within a few years of such an agreement being made, the productive power of the German group, or of the American or another group, would have increased, and this group would no longer be content with its former allocation. It would denounce the agreement, and if the other groups did not immediately submit, a new and more bitter struggle for markets would begin. In fact, this is the fate of all such agreements; and as the law of unequal development applies not only to particular industrial groups, but to the capital of different countries as a whole, economic agreements are only, so to speak, armistices in a continuous trade war between the finance-capital groups of different countries.

The economic war in itself can bring no solution. Therefore the finance-capital groups, through the State machinery of their respective countries, set up tariff barriers against their rivals, fix quotas on imports, try to arrange preferential trading agreements with other countries, strive to extend the territory within which they exercise their monopoly – and arm for the war in which victory will bring them at least a temporary superiority over their rivals.

Two world wars have in fact been the outcome of the concentration of wealth in the hands of finance-capital groups in each country. What is apparently a purely economic process – the concentration of production and of capital – leads to the terrible social calamity of war.

The Marxist approach to war is not pacifist. It condemns imperialist wars to hold down peoples fighting for their liberation, since these hold back the advance of humanity. Such wars it regards as unjust. But wars fought by peoples against imperialist conquest or for liberation from imperialist rule Marxism regards as just, as also civil wars waged by the people to end exploitation. It is only through the victory of the peoples against the exploiters that the conditions which produce war can be ended and thus war abolished for ever.

When the government of an imperialist country is waging an unjust war, the working class in that country must oppose the war by every possible means, and if it is strong enough bring down the government and take power, to end the war and begin the advance to socialism. This was the policy followed by the Russian workers in 1917.

The competitive struggle between rival imperialist groups results in general worsening of conditions. Technical rationalisation – labour-saving machinery – brings with it intense speeding up and unemployment. Wages are forced down to reduce costs and win or keep markets. The big monopoly concerns reduce the prices they pay for agricultural products. Social services are cut down, in order to save money for arms and other war preparations. Economic crises are deeper and more prolonged. Such was the experience in the period between the two world wars.

For all these reasons the class struggle and the struggle of the colonial peoples against the imperialists grow more acute. The imperialist stage of capitalism is an epoch not only of wars but also of revolutions.

But there is another feature of the imperialist stage of capitalism which Lenin brought out in his analysis. The monopolist groups in the imperialist countries are able to draw profits above the average from the exploitation of backward peoples. This is partly because of the low standard of living of these peoples; partly because of the terrible conditions forced on them by completely callous rulers and capitalists; and partly because of the fact that the products of machine industry can be exchanged with handicraft products at a very specially high rate of exchange. This does not refer to money, but to the actual goods. It will be remembered that the exchange value of any product is determined by the average socially necessary labour involved in its production. The socially necessary labour time, say in Britain, to produce one yard of cloth with machinery might be only one-tenth or one-twentieth of the time taken to produce one yard of cloth on a hand loom. But when the machine made cloth entered India, it exchanged against the value of one yard of Indian cloth, in other words, it exchanged in India at very much above its value in Britain. By the time raw materials or other Indian products equal to this higher value are brought back to Britain and sold, there is a much higher profit than if the yard of cloth had been sold in Britain. Even where the type of machinery is the same, different levels of skill produce their effect, and result in an extra profit. This extra profit, of course, applies to all transactions of this kind, not only to cloth, with the result that enormous fortunes are made by the finance-capital groups.

This extra profit arising from the exploitation of the colonial peoples has a special importance in relation to the labour movement. Marx had already pointed out that the British capitalist class, having been first in the field in selling machine-made products throughout the world, had been able to respond to the pressure of the British working class for better conditions, so far as the upper sections of skilled workers were concerned. Thus some sections of skilled engineers and cotton workers of Britain had secured far higher standards of living than workers in other countries; and along with this they tended to identify their interests with the capitalist exploitation of the colonies. Lenin showed that this occurred in each advanced industrial country when it reached the imperialist stage, and that sections of workers in a relatively privileged position, especially the leaders of these sections, tended to become "opportunists," that is, to come to terms with the capitalists on behalf of their own sections, without considering the conditions of the great mass of the workers in the country. This tendency became stronger as the imperialist stage developed, with the result that the leading sections of the labour and socialist movement became closely identified with the imperialist policy of the finance-capital group in their own country. During the First World War this was made clear by the association of the official labour movement everywhere (except in Russia, where the Bolsheviks remained Marxists) with "their own" imperialists in the war, instead of using the opportunity presented by the war to take power from the capitalist class.

This "opportunist" outlook (identification of their own interests with those of the ruling class) of the leaders of working class parties in many countries made necessary the formation, after the 1914-18 war, of Communist Parties, adhering to the outlook of Marxism and striving to win the working-class movement for Marxism.

In the imperialist stage the colonial struggle for liberation also becomes more determined and widespread. The conquest and capitalist penetration of a colonial country break up the old form of production, and destroy the basis on which large numbers of the people lived. Competition from Lancashire mills destroyed the livelihood of the Indian hand-loom workers, driving them back to agriculture and increasing the pressure on the land. In the imperialist stage the pressure on the whole people is increased by taxation to meet the interest on loans and to maintain the apparatus of imperial rule, both civil and military. As a result of this double pressure on the land and the forcing down of prices of colonial products by the big monopolies, poverty and literal starvation provide the basis for constant peasant struggles. In the towns industrial production is carried on under appalling conditions; working-class organisation is hampered and where possible suppressed. The middle classes, especially the *intelligentsia*, feel the restrictive bonds of imperial rule. The rising capitalists see their development restricted. Thus a wide movement for independence grows. The same process goes on, though in different conditions, in every colonial country. Since the Second World War the colonial liberation movement has made immense progress.

Marxists see these struggles as the inevitable result of

capitalist exploitation, and that they will only end with the overthrow of the imperialist groups. They therefore make common cause with the colonial peoples against their common enemy, the finance-capital group in the imperialist country.

The First World War, itself the result of the struggle between the finance-capital groups of the Great Powers, marked the beginning of what is known as *the general crisis of capitalism*. In 1917 the working class of Russia, led by the Bolshevik Party under Lenin and Stalin, overthrew the rule of the capitalists and landowners, and began to build the first socialist State in history. From that time, the world was divided into a socialist sector growing in strength and influence, and a capitalist sector in which all the contradictions of capitalism in its imperialist stage were more and more undermining the political and economic foundations of capitalist society.

Chapter 5

Class Struggles and The State

In Chapter 2 Marx's general theory of class struggle was described. Class struggles arise out of a form of production which divides society into classes, one of which carries out the actual process of production (slave, serf, wage-worker), while the other (slave-owner, lord, capitalist employer) enjoys a part of the product without having to work to produce it. But in addition to the two main classes in each epoch there are also other classes. In undeveloped ("colonial" or "semi-colonial") countries there are still today feudal landowners and peasants who are little more than serfs, alongside a developing capitalist class (besides foreign capitalists) and a growing working class.

The struggle between the classes helps man forward to a higher stage of production. When a successful revolution takes place, the higher form of production is brought in or widely extended. The way for the further development of capitalism in Britain was opened by the Cromwell revolution and the "Glorious Revolution" in 1688; the same service was rendered to France by the Great Revolution of 1789 and the subsequent revolutions.

Marx, however, was not content to state the facts in general terms: he closely examined the struggles of his day, in order to discover the *laws* of the struggle between classes.

This is not a question of the technical details of fighting. Marx saw that what was important for an understanding of social development was the analysis of the class forces which take part in the revolutionary movement that develops a new form of production. And it was possible for him to show, by examining particularly the revolutionary events in 1848 in many countries of Europe, that certain general features applied to all.

What are these general features or laws evident in revolutions?

In the first place, the revolutionary struggle is always conducted by the class which is coming to power in the new system of production, but not by it alone. For example, alongside of the rising capitalist class in the Great French Revolution of 1789, there were the peasantry – the producing class of feudalism – small traders, independent artisans and the rudiments of the working class of the future. All of these sections of the population took part in the revolutionary struggle against the ruling class of the old order, because, in spite of divergent interests, all of them realised that the old order meant continued repression, continued and increasing difficulties for them.

All subsequent experience has confirmed the conclusion drawn by Marx – that every real revolution which aims at overthrowing an existing ruling class is not a revolution only of the class which is to succeed it in power, but a revolution of all who are oppressed or restricted by the existing ruling class. At a certain stage of historical development the revolution is led by the capitalists against the feudal monarchy and landowners; but when the working class has developed it is able to lead all the sections taking part in the revolution. In other words, history shows that in every revolution wide sections of the people form an alliance against the main enemy; what is new is that in the revolution against the large landowners and capitalists the working class takes the lead in such an alliance.

The revolution which puts a new class in power to bring in a new system of production is only the high point of the continuous struggle between the classes, which is due to their conflicting interests in production. In the early stages of industrial capitalism, the conflicts are scattered, and are almost entirely on issues of wages and conditions in a particular factory. "But with the development of industry the proletariat not only increases in number; it becomes concentrated in greater masses, its strength grows, and it feels that strength more" (Marx, *Communist Manifesto*, 1848). The workers form trade unions, which develop into great organisations capable of carrying on the conflict on a national scale. They form co-operative societies to protect their interests as consumers. And at a relatively advanced stage they form their own political party, which is able to represent and lead the fight for their interests as a class.

How is the fight conducted?

Marx saw the aim of the working-class party as to prepare for and organise the overthrow of the ruling class of capitalists – to establish working class rule and build up a new system of production, socialism.

The process of preparation involved helping all forms of working-class organisation to develop, especially the trade unions, which increased the strength of the working class and made it "feel that strength more." It also involved helping every section of the workers which entered into any struggle for its immediate interests – for higher wages, better working conditions and so on. Through these struggles the workers often win better conditions; but "the real fruit of their battle lies, not in the immediate result, but in the ever-expanding union of the workers." Some critics interpret this statement by Marx to mean that Marxists do not want to improve conditions under capitalism, but are only concerned to prepare for revolution. This is not correct. Marx in fact worked, and Marxists at all times have worked, to improve conditions for the people as positive social gains.

What Marx was stressing in this passage was that these positive gains were not secure and left the capitalist system unchanged; but they helped to develop the strength of the working class for its ultimate aim – the ending of capitalism. For in the course of these struggles the workers become conscious of the fact that they are a class, with common interests as against the capitalist class. The working-class political party helps forward that development, and explains why, so long as capitalist production continues, the struggle between the classes must also go on, while economic crises and wars inflict terrible sufferings on the workers; but that the conflict and sufferings can be ended by changing the system of production, which, however, involves as a rule the forcible overthrow of the capitalist class.

This general conclusion, reached from past history, was reinforced by Marx's study of the State.

The State is sometimes thought of as parliament. But Marx showed that the historical development of the State had little to do with representative institutions; on the contrary, the State was something through which the will of the ruling class was imposed on the rest of the people. In primitive society there was no State; but when human society became divided into classes, the conflict of interests between the classes made it impossible for the privileged class to maintain its privileges without an armed force directly controlled by it and protecting its interests. "This public force exists in every State; it consists not merely of armed men, but of material appendages, prisons and repressive institutions of all kinds." (Engels, quoted by Lenin, *State and Revolution*, Ch. I.) This public force always has the function of maintaining the existing order, which means the existing class division and class privilege; it is always represented as something above society, something "impartial," whose only purpose is to "maintain law and order," but in maintaining law and order it is maintaining the existing system. It comes into operation against any attempt to change the system; in its normal, everyday working, the State machine arrests and imprisons "seditious" people, stops "seditious" literature, and so on, by apparently peaceful means; but when the movement is of a wider character, force is used openly by the police and, if necessary, the armed forces. It is this apparatus of force, acting in the interests of the ruling class, which is the essential feature of the State.

Is the State machine controlled by the Parliament or other representative institution of the country? So long as the representative institution of the country represents only the ruling class, it may appear to control the State machine. But when the Parliament or other institution does not adequately represent the ruling class, and attempts to carry through measures disturbing to the ruling class, the fact that it does not control the State machine soon becomes obvious. History is full of representative institutions which have attempted to serve the interests of a class other than the ruling class; they have been closed down, or dispersed by armed force where necessary. Where – as, for example, in Britain in Cromwell's time – the rising class has triumphed over the old order, it has not done so by mere votes in Parliament, but by organising a new armed force against the State, against the armed force of the old ruling class.

The class which is dominant in the system of production maintains its control of the State machine, no matter what happens in the representative institution. A change of real power therefore involves the use of force against the old State machine, whose whole apparatus of force is turned against the new class which is trying to change the system.

This conclusion reached by Marx from his study of past history is supported by many more recent historical events. The whole basis of fascism was the destruction by armed forces of all forms of representative institution.

The fact that the fascist organisation was a new form, and not merely the old form of State force, alters nothing in the main analysis. The Franco rebellion in Spain in 1936, against a constitutionally elected parliamentary government, shows how little control a representative institution has over the armed forces.

But how does the ruling class maintain its separate control of the State machine, and especially the armed forces which, on the surface and "constitutionally," are controlled by Parliament? The answer is to be found in the character of the State machine itself. In every country, the higher posts in the armed forces, in the judicial system, and in the administrative services generally, are held by members or trusted servants of the ruling class. This is assured by the system of appointment and promotion. However far democracy might go in the representative institution, there has been much experience to support the view that it was unable to penetrate into the tough core of the State machine. So long as no serious issues arise, the fact that the State machine is separated from the democratic Parliament is not obvious. But even in Britain we have the example of the mutiny at the Curragh in 1914, when officers refused to carry out an order to garrison Northern Ireland against the reactionary rebellion that was then being organised to prevent the operation of the Irish Home Rule Act that had been passed by Parliament.

So if the State machine works only to preserve the *status quo* and not against it, past experience suggested that no advance to a higher form of production is possible without the defeat of the State machine, no matter what representative institutions exist.

Nevertheless, Marx was always a supporter of democratic institutions. He saw them historically as one of the fields of the class struggle.

That is why Marx always stressed the importance of the fight for parliamentary democracy against the various forms of autocratic government existing in Europe during last century, and for the extension of democratic rights in countries where the autocracy had already been overthrown. At the same time, he considered that so long as the autocracy or the capitalist class remained in control of the State (in the meaning explained above) democracy is neither secure nor effective. It is only when the working class had succeeded in defeating and smashing the capitalist State machine that it could raise itself to the position of ruling class, and thereby "win the battle of democracy." In other words, the people's will could only prevail effectively when the armed barrier in its way – the capitalist State machine – had been destroyed.

But it is not enough to defeat and destroy the State machine of the former ruling class. It is necessary, Marx argued, for the working class to set up its own State machine – its own centralised apparatus of force – in order to complete the defeat of the capitalist class and to defend the new system against attacks from within and from without.

Moreover, it is necessary for the working class to set up its own form of government, which differs in important aspects from the form known in capitalist society, because its purpose is different. This became clear to Marx after the experience of the Paris Commune in 1871, the special features of which were that: it was "a working, not a parliamentary body, executive and legislative at the same time"; its members could be replaced by their electors at any time; "from the members of the Commune downwards, the public service had to be done at workmen's wages"; magistrates and judges were elected, and their electors could replace them at any time. The old standing army was replaced by a "National Guard, the bulk of which consisted of working men." The essence of these and other features of the Commune was to bring the governing apparatus and the machinery of force and repression nearer to the working class – to ensure its control by the working class, in contrast with the capitalist control which had in fact existed over the old machine. This new form of State was "winning the battle of democracy" – it was an enormous extension of the share taken by the common people in the actual control of their own lives.

Yet Engels, writing of the Paris Commune, said: "That was the Dictatorship of the Proletariat." Is there any contradiction between the two statements about the Commune: that it was a great extension of democratic control as compared with parliamentary democracy under capitalism; on the other hand, that it was a working-class dictatorship? No. They simply express two aspects of the same thing. In order to carry out the will of the overwhelming majority of the people, a "new and really democratic State" was set up, but this could only carry out the people's will by exercising a dictatorship, by using force against the minority who had been the class exercising its dictatorship and continued to use all means – from financial sabotage to armed resistance – against the people's will.

The later experiences of working-class revolution confirmed the deductions which Marx and Engels had drawn from the experience of the Commune in 1871. In the 1905 revolution in Russia, councils composed of delegates from working-class bodies were set up to organise and carry on the fight against the Tsar; and again in the March revolution of 1917 similar "soviets" (the Russian word for "council") were formed as soon as the revolutionary situation developed. Lenin saw that, with the great development of the working class since the Paris Commune, these delegate bodies, drawn in the first place from the factories (but also, as the struggle extended, from the soldiers and peasants), were the form in which the new working-class State would operate. The delegates were drawn directly from the workers, and could at any time be recalled by their electors; this meant that capitalist influences could play no part in decisions, and that therefore the real interests of the working class would be protected and advanced. At the same time, this could only be done by a dictatorship, resting on force, against the old ruling class, which used every means to undermine and destroy the new Soviet Government.

The real democracy of the working-class dictatorship was brought out by Marx in a passage in the *Communist Manifesto* of 1848: "All previous historical movements were movements of minorities, or in the interests of minorities. The proletarian movement is the self-conscious, independent movement of the immense majority, in the interest of the immense majority."

It is evident from what has been said above that Marx did not consider that the victory of the working-class revolution would at once end all class struggle. On the contrary, it merely marks a turning point in which the working-class for the first time has the State apparatus on its side instead of against it. Lenin told the Congress of Soviets in January, 1918, an incident which illustrates this point. He was in a train, and there was a conversation going on which he could not understand. Then one of the men turned to him and said: "Do you know the curious thing this old woman said? She said: 'Now there is no need to fear the man with the gun. I was in the woods one day and I met a man with a gun, and instead of taking the firewood I had collected from me, he helped me to collect some more'." The apparatus of force was no longer turned against the workers, but helped the workers; it would be turned only against those who tried to hold back the workers.

And such people, of course, continue to exist after the working class has taken power. The old ruling class, aided by the ruling class of other countries, gathers together such armed forces as it can raise and carried on open warfare against the working-class State. The Paris

Commune of 1871 was defeated in this way. The Germans released thousands of French prisoners taken in the war, and sent them to reinforce the French reactionaries at Versailles, outside Paris; and the reactionary army was able to take Paris from the Commune and carry out an appalling slaughter of those who had supported the Commune. Between 1918 and 1920, the Soviet Government in Russia had to face, not only armies of Tsarist supporters, but also invading armies of foreign powers – Britain, France and the United States included. In the second world war Soviet Russia had to face the Nazi invasion. History therefore confirms the conclusion made by Marx, that the working class would have to maintain its State organisation for a long period after it has taken power, in order to defend itself and to ensure its control during the period when it is reorganising the system of production on to a socialist basis.

The Paris Commune of 1871 and the Russian Soviet State established in 1917 were the first forms of working-class State. At the end of the Second World War the strength of the working-class movement and the existence of the powerful Soviet State made possible new forms of transition to socialism and new forms of working-class State. These are dealt with in the final chapter.

What exactly Marx meant by socialism and its higher stage, communism, is explained in the following chapter. But before leaving the subject of the class struggle and the State, Marx's view of the final outcome of the process must be stated. Class struggle, and with it the setting up of a State apparatus to protect the interests of the ruling class, came out of the division of human society into classes whose interests clashed in production. Class struggle and the State continue through history as long as human society remains divided into classes. But when the working class takes power, it does so in order to end the class divisions – to bring in a new form of production in which there is no longer any class living on the labour of another class; in other words, to bring about a classless society, in which all serve society as a whole. When this process has been completed (on a world scale), there will be no class conflict because there are no classes with separate interests and therefore there will be no need of a State – an apparatus of force – to protect one set of interests against another. The State will "wither away" – in one sphere after another it will not be required, and such central machinery as exists will be for the organisation of production and distribution. As Engels put it: "Government over persons is replaced by the administration of things and the direction of the processes of production."

Chapter 6
Socialist Society

Nowhere in Marx's writings is there to be found a detailed account of the new social system which was to follow capitalism. Marx wrote no "Utopia" of the kind that earlier writers had produced – writings based only on the general idea of a society from which the more obvious evils of the society in which they lived had been removed. But from the general laws of social development Marx was able to outline the principal features of the new society and the way in which it would develop.

Perhaps the most striking, although in a sense the most obvious, point made by Marx was that the organisation of the new society would not begin, so to speak, on a clear field. Therefore it was futile to think in terms of a socialist society "which has developed on its own foundations." It was not a question of thinking out the highest possible number of good features and mixing them together to get the conception of a socialist society, which we would then create out of nothing. Such an approach was totally unscientific, and the result could not possibly conform to reality.

On the contrary, an actual socialist society, like all previous forms of society, would only come into existence on the basis of what already existed before it; that is to say, it would be a society "just *emerging* from capitalist society, and which therefore in all respects – economic, moral and intellectual – still bears the birthmarks of the old society from whose womb it emerged."

In fact, it is the actual development within capitalist society which prepares the way for socialism, and indicates the character of the change. Production becomes increasingly social, in the sense that more and more people are associated in the making of every single thing; factories get larger and larger, and the process of production links together a very large number of people in the course of transforming raw materials into the finished article. There is greater and greater interdependence between people; the old feudal local ties and connections have long been broken by capitalism, but in its development capitalism has built new connections of a far wider character – so wide that every individual becomes more or less dependent on what happens to society as a whole.

But although this is the steady tendency of capitalist production, the fact is that the product, made by the co-operative work of society, is the property of an individual or group and not the property of society. The first step in building up a socialist society must therefore be so to organise production that society as a whole gets the benefit of the product which it has made; and this means that society as a whole must own the means of production – the factories, mines, machinery, ships, etc., which under capitalism are privately owned.

But this socialisation of the means of production itself takes place only on the basis of what the new society inherits from the old. And it is only the relatively large concerns which are so to speak ready to be taken over by society. Capitalist development has prepared them for this. There is already a complete divorce between the owners and the production process in such concerns; the only link is the dividend or interest paid to the shareholders. Production is carried on by a staff of workers and employees; the transfer of ownership to society as a whole does not alter their work. Therefore these large concerns can be taken over immediately.

But this is not the case with smaller enterprises owned by small manufacturers, small traders and retailers, small farmers – in which the owner plays an important part in production and management. As against the few hundred large shareholders in all the big companies, the "small" men in Britain number hundreds of thousands. It is the same in other countries, especially where capitalist agriculture has not developed and peasants form a large proportion of the population. From a practical standpoint, centralised administration of all these separate productive and distributive units is impossible. And there are also even more important social and political reasons why the "small" men should not be expropriated and their enterprises taken over at once by the State.

From a social standpoint, great numbers of these people and their families are doing essential work. Their conditions of existence have been restricted by the big monopoly concerns and by the difficulties of "small" men in a society dominated by wealth. Even though most of them have a capitalist and individualist outlook, in practice they stand to benefit from the socialist transformation of society. The problem is to carry through this transformation in such a way that the "small" men do benefit from it, and realise that they benefit from it, so that they become supporters of the new social system.

What practical steps in this direction can be taken? In relation to small agricultural producers, Engels wrote:

> "Our task will first of all consist in transforming their individual production and individual ownership into co-operative production and co-operative ownership, not forcibly, but by way of example, and by offering social aid for this purpose."

In the Soviet Union and other countries which are building Socialism this method of encouraging co-operation has been applied in agriculture. State farms and State machine and tractor stations have been used to show the benefits that large scale farming and the use of modern methods bring to the producers, and State aid in various forms has made the change from individual to collective farming easier. One productive unit takes the place of scores or hundreds of smaller ones; the small producers learn to produce in common, their individualist outlook gradually gives place to a collective outlook. Education and the amenities of life that are possible in a large collective farm hasten the process; the collective outlook leads on to a social outlook. In China very elementary forms of co-operation have been used to bring the peasants together as a start, leading on to more developed forms.

Co-operative methods have also been applied in bringing together individual craftsmen and small producers in industry. But they cannot be easily applied in the case of the scattered small manufacturers and distributors who exist in large numbers in every country. What methods then are possible? In the socialist countries the general principle has been to develop the socialist enterprises, while gradually absorbing the "small" men into the socialist network, partly by the inducement of better opportunities and partly by pressure of taxation. In China, however, where conditions made it possible and necessary to leave comparatively large manufacturing and trading businesses in the hands of their private owners, a completely new method of gradual transformation has been applied. On the basis of national sentiment and appreciation of the great advance for China made under the new regime, many of the capitalist owners were not unwilling to work with the Government, which for its part was careful to take into account the capitalists' personal interests at all stages in the process of transformation.

The main stages in this process were: (1) the Government entering into contracts with privately owned enterprises, buying their products at agreed prices, and in some cases supplying them with raw materials to be worked up; (2) joint ownership of particular enterprises by the capitalist owners and the State – the capitalists taking a fixed proportion of the profit; (3) joint ownership of whole sections of industry or trade by the capitalists and the State, the capitalists taking a fixed percentage (normally 5 per cent) on the agreed value of their assets; (4) full State ownership. In the first stage the owners managed their enterprises; in the second they shared management with representatives of the State; in the third the State took full responsibility for management, though in all suitable cases the former owners were kept on as managers or in other responsible positions.

Once power is in the hands of the working class, and they have taken over for the nation the larger enterprises – the "commanding positions", as Lenin called them – the subsequent transformation of smaller capitalist enterprises can be carried out gradually, without sharp conflict. But the possibility of this gradual transformation without sharp conflict depends on the extent to which the anti-socialist forces – the dispossessed owners of the larger enterprises, together with foreign imperialist interests – themselves resort to force.

The Soviet Union, the first socialist country, had to face not only internal enemies who wanted to return to the old order, but also, in the early years, actual invasion by the armed forces of fourteen capitalist States, followed by economic blockade and sabotage, and in 1941 the Nazi invasion. It was inevitable therefore that force had to be used to a greater extent than has been necessary for other countries that have since established Socialism. But it has been possible for later socialist transformations to be more peaceful and less painful, just because the Soviet people fought so hard, defeated all enemies, carried through vast industrial and social plans, and built the first socialist society in the world.

It has now been shown that, in the later period of Stalin's life, force was used not only against dangerous enemies of the Soviet Union but also against loyal supporters, and that alongside the general democratic advance of the people from Tsarist rule there grew up bureaucracy and Stalin's personal autocracy.

When Marx spoke of the working class becoming the ruling class, and thus "winning the battle of democracy", he was referring to the general democratic advance for the people, who would be no longer subject to the rule and conditions of life and work imposed by the former property-owning class. Such a general advance took place in the Soviet Union; even in backward Russia, which had no experience of democratic government, autocratic rule was replaced by democratic institutions and elected representative bodies. The great mass of the people for the first time won democratic rights which in some respects were even fuller than those in capitalist countries with established democratic forms – for example, in relation to working conditions and the administration of the social services.

But the full development of democracy was impossible in the conditions of struggle against both internal and external enemies which the Soviet Union had to face. Security organisations were essential in the long period when the Soviet Union was like a fortress actively besieged by surrounding capitalism and was also facing great internal difficulties. Strong, centralised leadership was also essential, and Stalin, an organiser and theoretician of outstanding ability, gained enormous prestige with every victory of the Soviet people. Hence arose the "cult" of Stalin, which developed into Stalin's personal control and gross violations of socialist principle and mass repressions through the State security organisations, as a result of whose intrigues similar injustices were committed also in the People's Democracies.

The cult of Stalin and its consequences did great harm in many spheres of Soviet life. But they did not change the nature of the socialist State and the immense human advances that had been made; and after Stalin's death measures were taken with the aim of restoring and strengthening socialist democracy in all the socialist countries, which are overcoming the evils of the Stalin period. The conditions in which the violations of democracy and justice arose will never be repeated: the socialist world is now too strong, and the lessons of the past have brought greater vigilance everywhere.

With power in the hands of the people, the building of the new society is essentially an *economic* and *social* process. The larger enterprises, the banks, the railways and other "commanding heights" of industry and trade are taken over, and form the economic base for further development. Small production and trade remain in private hands, and a more or less lengthy period has to be passed through before they are merged with State industry and trade. What working class power immediately achieves, therefore, is not Socialism; but it ensures that the country's development takes the direction of Socialism. It must be many years before all production and distribution is on a socialist basis, just as it must be many years before the whole population not only accepts Socialism but develops a really socialist outlook and way of life.

The transfer of the principal means of production from private ownership to ownership by society as a whole only prepares the ground. The next step is the conscious, planned development of the productive forces, in order that the rising needs of the people can be met.

It is a mistake to think that this development is only necessary in a backward industrial country such as Russia was in 1917. Marx was thinking of advanced

industrial countries when he wrote that after taking
power "the proletariat will use its political supremacy ...
to increase the total of productive forces as rapidly as
possible." And although these productive resources, for
example in Britain, have increased enormously since
Marx's day, the fact is that they are still backward in
relation to what scientific knowledge to-day makes
possible. They are backward because of the capitalist
system – because production is for the market, and as the
market is restricted under capitalism, the growth of the
productive forces is restricted, and in economic crises
productive forces, human as well as material, deteriorate
and may even be destroyed. They are backward too
because monopoly buys up technical inventions, and
prevents them from being widely used; because
production cannot be planned, and so there is no
systematic growth; because capitalism has kept
agriculture separate and backward; because capitalism
has to devote enormous resources for wars between rival
groups, wars against the colonial peoples; because
capitalism separates manual from mental work, and
therefore does not open the floodgates of invention;
because the class struggle absorbs an enormous amount
of human energy; because capitalism leaves millions of
the people without the education and training that would
enable them to play a full part in the development of
their country's resources.

Therefore the factories and the mines, the power-
stations and the railways, agriculture and fishing can
and must be reorganised and made more up-to-date, and
the whole people must be given a higher level of
education and training, so that a far higher level of
production can be reached. What is the object of this? To
raise the standard of living of the people.

One of the favourite arguments of the anti-socialists
used to be that if everything produced in Britain was
divided up equally, this would make very little difference

in the standard of living of the workers. Even if this were true – and it is not – it has absolutely nothing to do with Marx's conception of socialism. Marx saw that socialism would raise the level of production to undreamed-of heights. It is not merely because Tsarist Russia was backward that industrial production in the Soviet Union in 1955 was *twenty-five* times the 1913 level; even in industrial Britain an enormous increase could and would be made.

This increase in the level of production, and therefore in the standard of living of the people, is the material basis on which the intellectual and cultural level of the people will be raised.

But the whole development requires *planned production*. In capitalist society, new factories are built and production of any particular article is increased when a higher profit can be made by this increase. And it does not by any means follow that the higher profit means that the article in question is needed by the people. The demand may come from a tiny section of very rich people; or some exceptional circumstances may raise prices for one article. Where profit is the motive force, there can be only anarchy in production, and the result is constant over-production in one direction and under-production in another.

In a socialist society, where production is not for profit but for use, a plan of production is possible. In fact, it is possible even before industry is fully socialised. As soon as the main enterprises are socialised, and the others are more or less regulated, a plan of production can be made – a plan that grows more accurate every year.

So we see that Marx saw socialism as implying, in the economic field, ownership of the means of production by society as a whole; a rapid increase in the productive forces; planned production. And it is the character of the plan of production that contains the secret of why there cannot be any over-production under socialism in spite of the fact that the means of production are always being increased.

The national plan of production consists of two parts: the plan for new means of production — buildings, machinery, raw materials, etc. — and the plan for articles of consumption, not only food and clothing but also education, health services, entertainment, sport and so on, besides administration. So long as defence forces are required, these must also be provided for in the plan.

There can never be over-production, because the total output of articles of consumption is then allocated to the people — that is to say, total wages and allowances of all kinds are fixed to equal the total price of articles of consumption. There may, of course, be bad planning — provision may be made one year for more bicycles than the people want and too few boots. But such defects are easily remedied by an adjustment of the next plan, so that the balance is righted. It is always only a case of adjusting production between one thing and another — never of reducing total production, for total consumption never falls short of total production of consumption goods. As planned production of these rises, so does their planned distribution.

But they are not divided out in kind among the people. The machinery used is the distribution of money to the people, in the form of wages or allowances. As the prices of the consumption goods are fixed, the total wages and allowances paid can be made roughly equal to the total price of the consumption goods. There is never any discrepancy between production and consumption — the people are able to buy everything that is available. Increased production means increasing the quantity of goods available and therefore the quantity taken by the people.

The part played by prices in socialist society is often misunderstood. In the capitalist system, price fluctuations indicate the relation between supply and demand. If prices rise, this means the supply is too small; if prices fall, the supply is too great and must be reduced. Prices therefore act as the regulator of production. But in socialist society prices are simply a regulator of consumption; production goes according to plan, and prices are deliberately fixed, so that what is produced will be consumed.

How is the total output of consumption goods shared out among the people? It is a complete misconception to think that Marx ever held that the products would be shared out equally. Why not? Because a socialist society is not built up completely new, but on the foundations it inherits from capitalism. To share out equally would be to penalise everyone whose standard of living had been above the average. The skilled workers, whose work in increasing production is in fact more important for society than the work of the unskilled labourer, would be penalised. Equality based on the unequal conditions left by capitalism would therefore not be just, but unjust. Marx was quite clear on this point; he wrote: "Rights, instead of being equal, must be unequal ... Justice can never rise superior to the economic conditions of society and the cultural development conditioned by them."

Men who have just emerged from capitalist society are in fact unequal, and must be treated unequally if society is to be fair to them. On the other hand, society only has this obligation to them if they serve society. Therefore "he that does not work, neither shall he eat." And it follows from this that the man who does more useful work for society is rightly given a higher standard of living. The distribution of the total products available for consumption is therefore based on the principle: from each according to his ability, to each according to his work.

But socialist society does not remain at the level inherited from capitalism; it raises production each year, and at the same time it raises the technical skill and the cultural development of the people. And the inequality of wages – the fact that skilled and culturally developed people get more than the unskilled – acts as an incentive to everyone to raise his or her qualifications. In turn the higher skill means more production – there is more to go round, and this enables *everyone*'s standard of living to be raised. Inequality in a socialist society is therefore a lever by which the whole social level is raised, not, as in capitalism, a weapon for increasing the wealth of the few and the poverty of the many.

Did Marx consider that this inequality would be a permanent feature of the future society? No, in the sense that a stage would be reached when it was no longer necessary to limit what people got to a share proportionate to the service they render to society.

After all, to divide up the product according to work done or any other principle is to confess that there is not enough to satisfy everyone's needs. In capitalist society a family which is able to afford as much bread as all members of the family need does not share out a loaf on any principle: every member of the family takes what he or she needs. And when production in a socialist society has risen to such a height that all citizens can take what they need without anyone going short, there is no longer the slightest point in *measuring* and *limiting* what anyone takes. When that stage is reached, the principle on which production and distribution are based becomes: from each according to his ability, to each according to his needs.

It is the point at which this becomes possible that distinguishes communism from socialism. Socialism, as Marx used the term, is the first stage, when the means of production are owned by the people and therefore there is no longer any exploitation of man by man, but before planned socialist production has raised the country's output to such a height that everyone can have what he needs.

But the stage of communism implies much more than merely material sufficiency. From the time when the working class takes power and begins the change to socialism, a change also begins to take place in the outlook of the people. All kinds of barriers which under capitalism seemed rigid grow weaker and are finally broken down. Education and all opportunities for development are increasingly open to all children equally, no matter what the status or income of their parents may be. "Caste" differences soon lose their significance. Children learn to use their hands as well as their brains. And this equalisation of physical and mental work gradually spreads through the whole people. Everyone becomes an "intellectual," while intellectuals no longer separate themselves off from physical work.

Women are no longer looked on as inferior or unable to play their part in every sphere of the life of society. Special measures are taken to make it easier for them to work. Creches are established at the factories, in the blocks of flats, and so on, so that mothers can have greater freedom. The work of women in the home is reduced by communal kitchens, laundries and restaurants. There is no compulsion on women to work, but they are given facilities which make work easy for them.

The barriers between national groups are broken down. There are no "subject races" in a socialist society; no one is treated as superior or inferior because of his colour or nationality. All national groups are helped to develop their economic resources as well as their literary and artistic traditions.

Democracy is not limited to voting for a representative in parliament every five years. In every factory, in every block of flats, in every aspect of life, men and women are shaping their own lives and the destiny of their country. More and more people are drawn into some sphere of public life, given responsibility for helping themselves and others. This is a much fuller, more real democracy than exists in capitalist society, where wealth and privilege constantly influence the working of democratic institutions.

The difference between the town and the countryside is broken down. The workers in the villages learn to use machinery and raise their technical skill to the level of the town workers. Educational and cultural facilities formerly available only in the towns grown up in the countryside.

In a word, on the basis of the changes in material conditions which socialism brings, vast changes also take place in the development and outlook of men and women. They will be people with "an all-round development, an all-round training, people who will be able to do everything."

Above all, the self-seeking, individualist outlook bred by capitalism will have been gradually replaced by a really social outlook, a sense of responsibility to society; as Marx put it: "labour has become not only a means of living, but itself the first necessity of life." In that stage of society, Communist society, there will no longer be any need for incentives or inducements to work, because the men and women of that day will have *no other outlook* than playing their part in the further development of society.

Is this Utopian? It could only be regarded as Utopian by people who do not understand the materialist basis of Marxism, which has been touched on in Chapter 2. Human beings have no fixed characteristics and outlook, eternally permanent. In primitive tribal society, even in those forms of it which have survived to recent times, the sense of responsibility to the tribe is very great. In later times, after the division of society into classes, the sense of social responsibility was broken down, but still showed itself in a certain feeling of responsibility to the *class*. In capitalist society there is the most extreme disintegration of social responsibility: the system makes "every man for himself" the main principle of life.

But even within capitalist society there is what is known as "solidarity" among the workers – the sense of a common interest, a common responsibility. This is not an idea which someone has thought of and put into the heads of workers: it is an idea which arises out of the material conditions of working-class life, the fact that they get their living in the same way, working alongside each other. The typical grasping individualist, on the other hand, the man with no sense of social or collective responsibility, is the capitalist surrounded by competitors, all struggling to survive by killing each other. Of course, the ideas of the dominant class – competition and rivalry instead of solidarity – tend to spread among the workers, especially among those who are picked out by employers for special advancement of any kind. But the fundamental basis for the outlook of any *class* (as distinct from individuals) is the material conditions of life, the way it gets its living.

Hence it follows that the outlook of people can be changed by changing their material conditions, the way in which they get their living. No example could be better than the change which has been brought about in the outlook of the peasantry in the Soviet Union. Everyone who wrote of the peasant in Tsarist Russia described his self-seeking, grasping individualism. Critics of the revolution used to assert that the peasant could never be converted to socialism, that the revolution would be broken by the peasantry. And it is perfectly true that the outlook of the peasantry was so limited, so fixed by their old conditions of life, that they could never have been "converted" to socialism by arguments, or forced into socialism by compulsion. What these critics did not understand, as they were not Marxists, was that a model farm, a tractor station near them, would make them see in practice that better crops were got by large-scale methods. They were won for machinery and methods which could only be operated by breaking down their individual landmarks and working the land collectively. And this in turn broke down the separatism of their outlook. They settled down to a collective basis of living, and became a new type of peasantry – a collective peasantry, with a sense of collective responsibility, which is already some distance along the road to a social outlook.

When therefore the material basis in any country is socialist production and distribution, when the way in which all the people get their living is by working for society as a whole, then the sense of social responsibility so to speak develops naturally; people no longer need to be convinced that the social principle is right. It is not a question of an abstract moral duty having to establish itself over the instinctive desires of "human nature"; human nature itself is transformed by practice, by custom.

Up to this point we have not considered the implications of socialist or communist society covering the whole world. But a world system of socialist society will mean the end of wars. When production and distribution in each country are organised on a socialist basis, there will be no group in any country which will have the slightest interest in conquering other countries. A capitalist country conquers some relatively backward country to extend the capitalist system, to open up new chances for profitable investments by the finance-capital group; to get new contracts for railways and docks, perhaps for new mining machinery; to obtain new sources of cheap raw materials and new markets. Socialist societies will not make war because there is nothing they, or any groups within them, can gain from war.

For the same reason no socialist state is in the least interested in holding back any backward country. On the contrary, the more every country develops its industry and cultural level, the better it will be for all the other socialist countries; the higher the standard of living throughout the world, the richer the content of life. Therefore those socialist countries which are industrially advanced help the more backward countries to develop. This principle is being operated today in the help given by the Soviet Union to industrially backward China, India and other countries.

In such a world socialist system the further advance that man could make defies the imagination. With all economic life planned in every country, and a world plan co-ordinating the plans of each separate country, with scientific discoveries and technical inventions shared out at once between all countries, with the exchange of every form of cultural achievement, man would indeed take giant's strides forward.

Towards what? Marx never attempted to foretell, because the conditions are too unknown for any scientific forecast. But this much is clear: with the establishment of communism throughout the world, the long chapter of man's history of class divisions and class struggles will have come to an end. There will be no new division into classes, because in a communist society there is nothing to give rise to it. The division into classes at a time when men's output was low served to provide organisers and discoverers of higher productive forces; the class division continued to fulfil this function, and under capitalism it helped the concentration of production and the vast improvements in technique.

But at the stage when man has equipped himself with such vast productive forces that only a few hours' work a day is necessary, the division into classes can well end, and must end. From that point on, man will resume his struggle with nature, but with the odds on his side. No longer trying to win nature with magic, or avert natural disasters with prayer, no longer blindly groping his way through class struggles and wars, but sure of himself, confident of his power to control the forces of nature and to march on – that is man in communist society as pictured by Marx.

Chapter 7

The Marxist View of Nature

The point has already been made that Marxism regards human beings, and therefore human society, as a part of nature. Man's origin is therefore to be found in the development of the world; man developed out of previous forms of life, in the course of whose evolution thought and conscious action made their appearance. This means that matter, reality that is not conscious, existed before mind, reality that is conscious. But this also means that matter, external reality, exists independently of the mind. This view of nature is known as "materialism."

The opposite view, the view that the external world is not real, that it has existed only in the mind, or in the mind of some supreme being, is known as idealism. There are many forms of idealism, but all of them are based on the belief that mind, whether human or divine, is the primary reality and that matter, if it has any reality at all, is secondary.

To the Marxists, as Engels put it, "the materialist world outlook is simply the conception of nature as it is, without any reservations." The external world is real, it exists independently of whether we are conscious of it or not, and its motion and development are governed by laws which are capable of being discovered and used by man, but are not directed by any mind.

Idealism, on the other hand, because it regards matter, external reality, as having only secondary reality, if indeed it is in any sense real, holds that we can never know reality, that we can never understand the "mysterious way" of the world.

Why is the controversy of materialism *versus* idealism

of importance? Because it is not just a question of speculation and abstract thought; it is, in the last analysis, a question of practical action. Man does not only observe external Nature: he changes it, and himself with it.

Secondly, the materialist standpoint also means that what mind is conscious of is external reality; ideas are abstractions drawn from reality, they have their origin in external reality. Of course this does not mean that all ideas are *true*, are correct reflections of reality; the point is that actual experience of reality is the test of whether they are correct or not.

The idealist, on the other hand, believes in eternally valid principles, and does not feel concerned in making them fit reality. An example of this in current affairs is the standpoint of absolute pacifism. The completely logical pacifist ignores the real world round him; it is a matter of no importance to him that in reality, in the actual experience of life at the present day, force is a fact that cannot be conjured away by wishing; that in reality, in our actual experience, non-resistance to force brings more force, more aggression and brutality. The fundamental basis of such absolute pacifism is an idealist view of the world, a disbelief in external reality, even if the pacifist concerned is not conscious that he has any such philosophical outlook.

Marxism, therefore, bases all its theories on the materialist conception of the world, and from this standpoint it examines the world, it tries to discover the laws which govern the world and – since man is a part of reality – the laws which govern the development of human society. And it tests all its discoveries, all its conclusions, by actual experience, rejecting or modifying conclusions and theories which, to use the simplest phrase, do not fit the facts.

This approach to the world (always including human society) reveals certain general features, which are real, and not imposed by the mind; the Marxist view is entirely scientific, drawn from reality, and is not a "system" invented by some clever thinker. Marxism sees the world as material, and finds that it has certain characteristics which are covered by the terms "dialectical." The phrase "dialectical materialism," which expresses the Marxist conception of the world, is sometimes regarded as mysterious. But it is not really mysterious, because it is a reflection of the real world, and it is possible to explain the word "dialectical" by describing ordinary things which everyone will recognise.

In the first place, nature or the world, including human society, is not made up of totally distinct and independent things. Every scientist knows this, and has the very greatest difficulty in making allowances for even the important factors which may affect the particular thing he is studying. Water is water; but if its temperature is increased to a certain point (which varies with the atmospheric pressure) it becomes steam; if its temperature is lowered, it forms ice; all kinds of other factors affect it. Every ordinary person also realises, if he examines things at all, that nothing, so to speak, leads an entirely independent existence; that everything is dependent on other things.

In fact, this interdependence of things may seem so obvious that there may not appear to be any reason for calling attention to it. But, in fact, people do not always recognise the interdependence of things. They do not recognise that what is true in one set of circumstances may not be true in another; they are constantly applying ideas formed in one set of circumstances to a quite different set of circumstances. A good example is "gunboat" diplomacy. In the earlier days of imperialism, the sending of a gunboat to cow a local chieftain was usually enough. But now that the colonial system is challenged, "gunboat" diplomacy no longer works, much to the disappointment of the imperialist "Blimps."

The dialectical approach also sees that nothing in the world is really static, that everything is moving, changing, either rising and developing or declining and dying away. All scientific knowledge confirms this. The earth itself is in constant change. It is even more obvious in the case of living things. Therefore it is essential to any really scientific investigation of reality, that it should see this change, and not approach things as if they were eternally fixed and lasting.

Again, why is it essential to bring out this feature of reality, which is so obvious when it is stated? Because in practice this is not the approach men make to reality, especially to human society, and for that matter to individual men and women. Many people believe that production for profit is a permanent feature of human society. And, in fact, the conception that "as it was, so it will be" is to be met with almost everywhere, and is a constant barrier to the development of individuals and of society.

There is a further point arising from the clear realisation that everything is changing, developing or dying away. Because this is so, it is of supreme practical importance to recognise the stage reached by each thing that concerns us. The farmer is well enough aware of this when he is buying a cow; the buyer of a house has it well in mind; in fact, in the simpler practical things of life no one ignores the general law. But it is unfortunately not so well appreciated in regard to human institutions, especially the system of production and the ideas that go with it. However, this is a point that is developed later on.

The interdependence of things, and the fact that things are always in a process of change, have been referred to as obvious features of reality. The third feature which is included in the "dialectical" approach to reality is not quite so obvious, although it is easy enough to recognise that it is true once it is stated.

This feature is: the development that takes place in things is not simple and smooth, but is, so to speak, broken at certain points in a very sharp way. The simple and smooth development may take place for a very long time, during which the only change is that there is more of a particular quality in the thing. To take the example of water again: while the temperature is being raised the water remains water, with all the general characteristics of water, but the amount of heat in it is increasing. Similarly, while the temperature is being reduced the water remains water, but the amount of heat in it is decreasing.

However, at a certain point in this process of change, at boiling or freezing point, a sudden break occurs; the water completely changes its qualities; it is no longer water, but steam or ice. This feature of reality is particularly evident in chemistry, where less or more of a particular constituent completely changes the character of the result.

In human society, gradual changes take place over a long period without any fundamental change in the character of society; then a break takes place, there is a revolution, the old form of society is destroyed, and a new form comes into existence and begins its own process of development. Thus within feudal society, which was production for local consumption, the buying and selling of surplus products led to the production of things for the market and so on to the beginnings of capitalist production. All of this was a gradual process of development; but at a certain point the rising capitalist class came into conflict with the feudal order, overthrew it, and transformed the whole character of production; capitalist society took the place of feudalism and began a more tempestuous development.

The fourth feature of dialectics is the conception of what causes the development which, as we have already seen, is universal. The dialectical approach to things shows that they are not simple, not completely of one character. Everything has its positive and its negative side; everything has within it features that are developing, becoming more dominant, and features that are passing away, becoming less dominant. One feature is always expanding, the other resisting that expansion. And it is the conflict between these opposites, the struggle of the rising factor to destroy the domination of the other, and the struggle of the dominant factor to prevent the other factor from developing, which is the content of the whole process of change which ends ultimately in a violent break.

This is most clearly seen in human society. At each historical stage there has been division into classes, one of which was developing and one declining. It was the case in feudal society, with capitalism developing in the germ and, as it developed, coming more and more into conflict with feudalism. It is the same in the capitalist period, with the working class as the rising factor that "has the future in its hands." Capitalist society is not all of one kind; as capitalists develop, so do workers. The conflict between these classes develops. It is this conflict, this "contradiction" within capitalism, and the actual struggles which arise from the division into classes, which ultimately lead to the sharp break, the revolutionary change in society.

It is now possible to put together the various ideas covered by the phrase "dialectical materialism." It is the view which holds that reality exists apart from our consciousness of it; and that this reality is not in isolated fragments, but interdependent; that it is not static but in motion, developing and dying away; that this development is gradual up to a point, when there is a sharp break and something new appears; that the development takes place because of internal conflict, and the sharp break is the victory of the rising factor over the dying factor.

It is this conception of the world, including human society, that sharply distinguishes Marxism from all other approaches to reality. Of course, dialectical materialism is not something standing above reality – an arbitrarily invented outlook into which the world must fit. On the contrary, it claims to be the most accurate representation of the world, and to be drawn from the accumulated knowledge and experience of man. It is in the mind of the Marxist because it is in the world outside; it is the real "shape of things."

The discoveries of science are more and more confirming that this is so; scientists who approach nature from the dialectical standpoint find that it helps the discovery of new facts, explains things which seemed inexplicable. But in the present stage of human development the outlook of dialectical materialism is of the greatest importance in relation to human society.

The examples given earlier in this chapter serve to show the difference in outlook between the Marxist and the non-Marxist in connection with the development of society and the ideas that spring from this development. There are other examples in other chapters. But the question of the nature of reality is of such practical importance in the life and actions of men and women that it is worth closer study.

It was noted above that the materialist outlook means that matter, external reality, is regarded as primary, and mind as secondary, as something that develops on the basis of matter. It follows from this that man's physical existence, and therefore the ways in which it is preserved, come before the ideas which man forms of his own life and methods of living. In other words, practice comes before theory. Man got himself a living long before he began to have ideas about it. But also the ideas, when he developed them, were associated with his practice; that is to say, theory and practice ran together. And this was not only in the early stages, but at all stages. The practical ways in which men get their living are the basis of their ideas. Their political ideas rise from the same root; their political institutions are formed in the practice of preserving the system of production, and not at all on the basis of any abstract principles. The institutions and ideas of each age are a reflection of the practice in that age. They do not have an independent existence and history, developing, so to speak, from idea to idea, but they develop when the material mode of production changes. A new custom takes the place of the old custom, and gives rise to new ideas.

But old ideas and institutions persist, alongside the new. Ideas which develop from the feudal system of production, such as respect for the monarch and the nobility, still play an important part in capitalist Britain. There are ideas developed from the capitalist system of production; some are modifications of old forms, such as respect for the wealthy irrespective of noble birth. Then there are the socialist ideas, derived essentially from the fact that production under capitalism becomes more and more social in character, more collective and interdependent. These three sets of ideas are current in present-day society, and no one of them is finally and absolutely true, valid for all eternity.

This, however, does not mean that Marxism regards them all as equally unreal. On the contrary, Marxism sees the feudal ideas as completely past, the capitalist ideas as declining, the socialist ideas as becoming valid. Or rather, at this stage not only becoming. For since November, 1917, it has been possible to test socialist ideas from actual experience: to prove that they fit reality. The main idea, that even the vast and complex modern machinery of production can be organised for use and not for profit, has been confirmed in practice. Experience has shown that this means also an enormous increase in production, the abolition of crises, and a continuous rise in the standard of living of the people. In other words, the socialist ideas, scientifically developed by Marx from the observed facts of economic and social development, remained, so to speak, a scientific hypothesis until 1917; now experience has confirmed them as true.

The conscious action of the Russian Communist Party, whose outlook was Marxist, brought about the overthrow of the old system and the establishment of the new. From that point on, the Russian people – overwhelmingly non-Marxist in their outlook – began to experience the new system, to become socialists *in practice*. On such a basis the conscious educational work of the theoretical socialists bore quick fruit, and the combination of practice and education is rapidly transforming the outlook of the whole people.

It should be made clear that Marxism does not claim more for its view of the world, dialectical materialism, than that this approach helps the investigator in every field of science to see and understand the facts. It tells us nothing about the details, which must be the subject of special study in each field. Marxism does not deny that a considerable body of scientific truth can be built up on the basis of studying the facts in isolation. But it claims that when they are examined in their interdependence, in their development, in their change of quantity into quality, in their internal contradiction, the scientific truth that emerges is infinitely more valuable, more *true*, and therefore more useful to society.

And this holds good also in the science of society. The study of individual men and women, or even of a whole society at one time and place, can give conclusions of only very limited value; they cannot be applied to other groups, or even to the same society at another time. What gives the Marxist study of society its special value is that it deals with society not only as it exists here and now (this is of course essential), but as it has existed in the past and as it is developing as the result of its internal contradictions. This gives men and women the first chance of consciously fitting their actions to a process that is actually taking place, a movement that, as Marx said, is "going on before our own eyes" if we care to see it. It gives us a guide to our actions which cannot be provided by any abstract principles or views which in fact represent some static outlook of the past.

Chapter 8

A Guide to Action

In one of his early works Marx wrote: "The philosophers have only *interpreted* the world in various ways; the point, however, is to *change* it". To Marx this was the essence of his view of the world – "Marxism" was not a mere academic science, but knowledge to be used by man in changing the world.

It was not enough to know that capitalism was only a passing phase and that it must be succeeded by Socialism, for this would not happen by itself, as a result of purely economic changes. However many crises developed, however much suffering was caused by capitalism, there was no point at which capitalism would automatically turn into socialism as water turns into ice when its temperature falls to 32° Fahrenheit. Humanity does not make the leap from one system of production to another except as the result of human action. Marxism, scientific socialism, draws from the experience of mankind the knowledge which can guide human action to that end.

Marx's view of the general type of action that changes society is already clear from Chapter 2: it is class struggle, at this stage the struggle of the working class against the capitalist class. But this general formula has to be filled in from actual experience, and applied to the conditions in each country at each stage of development.

Marx was continually working on this problem, not in an abstract way, but by examining what was actually taking place, and helping to build up the various kinds of working-class organisation on which he considered that all future human advance must depend. The famous

Communist Manifesto of 1848 was a manifesto of the
Communist League, the organisation in which Marx was
active for many years; the "International Workingmen's
Association," now known as the First International, was
founded by his efforts in 1864. Marx was closely in touch
with the British labour movement of his day, as well as
with the working-class movements in other countries.

In those days only a tiny fraction of the working class
was organised even in trade unions and co-operatives,
and in no country was there a working class party of any
size or influence. In most countries the working class
itself was hardly formed. Outside of Britain, capitalist
industry was only in its early stages, and in many
countries the rising capitalist class was still striving to
establish itself against the feudal aristocracy or its
survivals.

Towards the end of last century, working-class
political parties developed in a number of European
countries and won representation in the Parliaments; in
Britain, the Labour Party was formed after the turn of
the century, though its leaders were Radical rather than
socialist in outlook.

At the beginning of this century, when capitalism
reached its imperialist stage described in Chapter IV,
and "the epoch of wars and revolutions" opened, the
strategy and tactics of the class struggle had to be
developed further than was possible when Marx and
Engels lived. This application of Marxism to the period
of imperialism was carried out by Lenin.

In this period, Lenin showed, the old type of working-
class political party whose activity was almost exclusively
parliamentary and propagandist was inadequate. The
ending of capitalism was on the agenda; this required a
new type of party, one which combined the
parliamentary struggle with the struggle in the factories
and streets, one which aimed to lead the working class
towards the ending of capitalism and the building of

socialism.

Marx had repeatedly stressed the point that the class which overthrows a former ruling class depends on help from other sections of the people. The working class is not living in a vacuum; there is a very definite and real world round it, including other classes and sections of classes which vary from time to time and from country to country. The problem of strategy for a working-class party of the new type was the problem of winning not only the working class but also other sections of the people for the joint struggle against what in each country, at a particular time, was the main enemy of social advance.

The theory of the alliance of the working class with other sections against the main enemy, worked out in practice by Lenin in Russian conditions, has been of great significance in the further development of Marxism as a guide to working-class action.

The working class is the only consistent fighter against capitalism; it grows as capitalism extends, and is directly exploited by the capitalist class. Therefore the conception of an alliance against the capitalist class necessarily implies that the working class is the core of the alliance, the leading force. But the working class *needs* the alliance, all the more because when it fights the capitalist class the other sections gravitate either to the working class or to the capitalists. To win a section for alliance with the working class is to deprive the capitalists of that section's support.

Conditions become more favourable for an alliance between the workers and other sections against the main enemy of social advance, because in the monopoly stage of capitalism economic (and therefore political) power is more and more concentrated in the hands of small and very rich groups. It is true that the capitalist class has always had richer and less rich individuals in it; but in the stage of world-wide monopolies the monopoly capitalists are divided from the mass of smaller capitalists by a great gulf. The interests of the monopolists in extending their grip on industry and trade, in conquering new territory to exploit, and in dealing with their rival groups in other countries (dividing up markets with them, making price-fixing agreements, or fighting them with tariffs and even war) come into direct conflict with the interests of the small shopkeepers and small employers. They feel that they are being squeezed out of existence by the monopolists. On one issue after another – at first only as individuals, but sometimes also as whole sections – the small shopkeepers and small employers and farmers come to regard the monopolists as their "main enemy".

It is important to realise that this opposition develops not only on direct economic grounds. Economic monopoly, with its inevitable drive against the working class and the colonial peoples as well as against the smaller capitalists, tends also towards reactionary policies both at home and abroad. The smaller capitalists and the middle classes, professional workers and a large part of the *intelligentsia*, brought up in the liberal and democratic traditions associated with earlier capitalist periods, turn against the monopolists who violate these traditions. A clear example of this was the widespread opposition to the open, unrestricted dictatorship of fascism, which destroyed all democratic organisations and institutions and violated the most widely accepted humanitarian principles.

In these circumstances, when the fascists were seen by very wide circles as the main enemy in the way of peace and social advance, the interests of the workers and middle sections coincided, and it became possible to form a wide alliance – a "People's Front" – against the fascists.

There cannot be any real alliance except on issues on which the interests of the workers coincide with the interests of other sections of the people. It is not a question of either the workers or their allies abandoning their own special interests, or deceiving their partners in the alliance as to their real aims. The essence of the class alliance is that for the time being, in the special circumstances, the interests of the allies are identical. It was this that brought the Spanish workers, peasants, middle classes, smaller capitalists and nationalist groups into alliance in 1936 against the big landowners and bankers and foreign invaders associated with General Franco.

History shows many examples too of a "National Front" embracing almost all sections of the people for struggle against foreign conquerors or invaders, as in the Second World War. The "National Front" is always evident in the struggles of the colonial peoples for liberation from foreign imperialist rule. At first, these national liberation struggles are usually led by the rising capitalists. But the development of capitalism in a colonial country, together with the operations of the foreign imperialists, creates a working class; and as this grows in numbers and becomes organised, it takes an increasing part in leading the struggle for liberation. The formation of Marxist parties helps forward this process, which is further quickened by the general experience that a part of the capitalists formerly associated with the liberation movement comes to terms with the imperialists and sides with them against the people.

The case of China can be taken to illustrate this. In 1911 the "bourgeois" revolution reached a decisive stage against the old feudal rulers supported by the foreign imperialists. By the 1920s the working class in the industrial cities and ports had developed considerable strength and organisation; in 1921 the Communist Party was formed. The principal force in the national liberation movement throughout this period was the party formed in 1912 by Sun Yat-sen, the Kuomintang;

but the shock force against the foreign imperialists became more and more the working class, which conducted great strikes and demonstrations in industrial centres through 1924, 1925 and 1926. After Sun Yat-sen's death in 1925, the Kuomintang armies – with the full support of the working class and the Communist Party – marched northwards from Canton with the programme of unifying China and carrying through social reforms. In April 1927, however, Chiang Kai-shek, the military leader of the Kuomintang armies, came to terms with the foreign imperialists, and turned against the Communist Party and the working class. From that time on the national liberation movement was led not by the Kuomintang but by the Communist Party; although at certain stages of the later struggle against the Japanese invaders a common national front was again restored.

The theory of the alliance of the working class with other sections of the people against the main enemy was drawn from the actual experience of the struggle both in capitalist and in colonial or semi-colonial countries; in fact, Marxist theory is a generalisation from experience, and is, like all scientific theory, developed or modified by further experience. In the course of the Second World War, and particularly after its termination, new experiences in many countries led to extremely important new developments of the theory of allies and of the strategy of the working class in the struggle to win socialism.

In the European countries occupied by the Nazi German imperialists during the war, there arose a national resistance movement drawing its strength from the working class and led by the Communist Party, but embracing all sections of the people who were not "Quislings" or traitors to their country. Chief among these traitors were the big landowners and capitalists, who came to terms with the Nazi conquerors in order to retain their privileges and profits. On the other hand, the bulk of the smaller capitalists and most middle class sections joined with the working class and peasants against the Nazi occupation and for the liberation of their country.

With the military defeat of the Nazis and the liberation of the occupied countries, this national alliance in each country became the basis for the provisional government, within which the working-class parties – Communist and Social Democratic – had considerable strength. Local committees, formed on the basis of the national alliance, but closer to the mass of working people, also strengthened working-class influence, and broke down the local influence of the former big landowners and capitalists. The programme of the governments, because of these factors, were progressive, involving in Eastern Europe taking over the big landed estates and distributing this land to the peasants, and the establishment of democratic government nationally and locally, in countries whose past had been feudal and fascist dictatorship. This was the first stage of a "People's Democracy" in the countries of Eastern Europe.

The Communist Parties of those countries saw that this new type of Government and State could be developed into an instrument for carrying through the change from capitalism to socialism. On the one hand, the leaders of the capitalist and peasant parties, as well as some of the Social Democratic leaders, had no liking for fundamental social changes, and regarded the initial programme of the government, which they had accepted under popular pressure, as the limit of change. On the other hand, the bulk of working people in town and country, elated by the victory over fascism and their own old rulers, and for the first time given full political rights, fully supported the more far-reaching measures put forward by the Communist Party. This led to the merging of the Social Democratic with the Communist

Parties, forming a single party of the working class on the basis of Marxism.

Through a series of parliamentary measures supported by an overwhelming majority of the people, industry and trade were taken over by the State and a planned economy developed; the turn was made towards collective agriculture; the leading positions in the armed forces, civil service, nationalised industry and trade were filled by advocates of socialism, replacing supporters of capitalism.

This transition to socialism through People's Democracy was made possible and aided throughout by the socialist Soviet Union. After the Nazi armies had been smashed by the Soviet army and the national liberation movement in each country, the provisional government set up by the latter was able to carry through the agreed programme without the threat of imperialist intervention such as the Soviet Government in its early days had to cope with. Instead of being isolated and having to build up socialism in a hostile world, as the Soviet Government has had to do, the People's Democracies, secure from armed intervention, received help in food, materials and machinery from the Soviet Union, besides being able to draw on the immense fund of experience accumulated in the Soviet Union in the socialist solution of economic, political and social problems. Reliance on the Soviet Union also had its negative side, due to distortions of socialist principle to which reference has already been made, and to the tendency to copy Soviet methods without giving enough consideration to the conditions in each country. But this does not alter the truth that the foundations of Socialism were laid in these countries thanks to Soviet aid.

A development somewhat similar to that of the People's Democracies took place in China after the defeat of the Japanese in the Second World War. The armed struggle between Chiang Kai-shek and the

Communist Government established in north-western China was to some extent suspended during the war, in response to the Communist call for national unity against the Japanese. But when the war ended, the efforts of the Communist Party to bring about a united democratic government for China were resisted by Chiang Kai-shek, who with great military and financial resources supplied by the United States Government resumed armed struggle against the Communist Government. By 1949 Chiang Kai-shek, defeated and discredited, had fled to Taiwan (Formosa), and the Communist Party summoned a "People's Consultative Council" to set up a new government. The Chinese People's Republic was formed; its government was based on alliance between the working class, the peasants, the urban petty bourgeoisie, and the "national" (i.e. patriotic) capitalists, as opposed to the "bureaucratic" or monopoly capitalist group associated with Chiang Kai-shek. Thus the nation was united against the small group of traitors who had amassed fortunes at the expense of the people and had become tools of the United States imperialists; the land of the landowners was distributed among the peasants; industry and trade were revived, under Government control but mainly in private hands; democratic institutions were set up in town and country. The People's Republic was firmly established in a united and democratic China, and the economic transformation of the country – the foundation for the advance in the direction of socialism – had begun, under a broad-based government of national unity led by the Communist Party.

These experiences in Eastern Europe and in China show that new conditions have arisen for solving the problem of the advance to socialism. In the general crisis of capitalism, the monopolist groups are more and more driven to desperate measures in their efforts to maintain their robbery of the peoples. Fascism, war, and the forcing down of conditions for working people – that is one side of the picture. The other side is the growth of the socialist sector in the world, the growing resistance of the workers and colonial peoples, and the ability of the Communist Parties, with their Marxist outlook, to draw into the struggle against the monopolists not only the working class but the majority of the people. Both in capitalist and in colonial countries, the monopolists find themselves more and more isolated, while the alliance of the people against them grows wider and stronger in the fight for peace, national independence, democracy and a better life.

But victory over the monopolists requires as its first condition the defeat of opportunism within the working-class movement. For the experience of history and of the working class, embodied in Marxism, shows that the road to a new stage of human society lies through class struggle, not collaboration with the rulers of an outworn society. No "bi-partisan" policy either at home or abroad, but only a working-class policy and an active struggle *directed against the policy of the monopolists* can give the working class the irresistible strength and determination to carry through its historic mission.

The fundamental lessons drawn by Marx and Lenin from past experience remain valid. The advance to a higher form of society can only be won in struggle against capitalism and imperialism; it can only be maintained by continuing that struggle against both the remnants of the old ruling class at home and the foreign imperialists. The transformation of society can only be realised through the winning of political power. This requires an alliance of working people led by the working class, guided by a revolutionary party which has mastered the lessons drawn by Marxism from the class struggle itself.

The road to Socialism is not an easy one. But the difficulties are not today so hard to overcome, because of the profound changes in the world brought about, in the first place, through the Russian revolution of November 1917. A thousand million people – more than a third of the human race – have already broken with the feudal and capitalist past, and are building up a new life based on the principle that, as Marx and Engels put it in the Communist Manifesto, "the free development of each is the condition for the free development of all."

All the experience of recent years has been summed up in the Statement issued by the meeting of Communist and Workers' Parties in Moscow in November 1960: "The chief result of these years is the rapid growth of the might and international influence of the world socialist system, the vigorous process of disintegration of the colonial system under the impact of the national-liberation movement, the intensification of class struggles in the capitalist world, and the continued decline and decay of the world capitalist system".

The statement says that the main content of our epoch is the transition from capitalism to socialism; this however is no automatic process: it is a time of struggle between the two opposing social systems, of socialist revolutions and national-liberation revolutions, the breakdown of imperialism and abolition of the colonial system, the transition of more peoples to the socialist path, the triumph of socialism and communism on a world scale.

In this period the main trend and main features of the development of society are determined not by imperialism, but by the world socialist system and the forces fighting against imperialism. The united strength of these forces can prevent the imperialists from launching a new world war. In these conditions the aim of Communists in all countries is not only to abolish exploitation and poverty throughout the world and thus end all possibility of war, but also to deliver mankind from the nightmare of a new world war already in our time.

In the capitalist countries, conditions are favourable for unity of the working class and broad sections of the population in the struggle against the monopolists, for peace, democracy and the vital interests of the people; and in a number of capitalist countries there is the opportunity to win State power and realise the socialist revolution without civil war – though the resort to violence may come from the exploiting class.

Finally, the Statement records the growth of Communist Parties in 87 countries, with a total membership of 36 million, and stresses the need for communist unity on the basis of the teachings of Marx and Lenin as the guarantee of new victories in the struggle for a happy future for the whole of mankind.

In the years following the Second World War the imperialist powers had hopes of checking this process by force, and perhaps even of crushing the socialist countries. This was the essence of the North Atlantic Treaty Organisation and the huge rearmament programmes in the United States and the West European capitalist countries, together with the re-arming of Western Germany. It was the essence of the extension of this imperialist alliance to the Far East, in the South East Asia Treaty Organisation; and of the British attempts to build up a similar Middle East alliance through the Baghdad Pact. It was the essence of the attempts made by the most aggressive United States imperialists to develop the Korean war into war against People's China; as it was the essence of the United States intervention in the Congo, its frustrated attempts to crush the successful revolution in Cuba and its indirect attacks on the national liberation and progressive movements in Latin America, and above all its full-scale aggression against the Vietnamese people. Alongside these international capitalist efforts to hold back the tide, Britain has used force in Malaya, Kenya, British Guiana, Cyprus and Egypt. Holland tried unsuccessfully to hold back the liberation movement in Indonesia; France, defeated in Vietnam, made fruitless attempts to hold back the movement in Morocco and Tunisia, and engaged in a prolonged struggle in Algeria.

It is necessary to stress these facts in order to show that the Marxist thesis that monopoly capitalism drives to war has been by no means outdated. The class approach of Marxism enables the working class to see clearly, through all war propaganda, the forces driving to war and the forces fighting for peace. On the one hand, the imperialist groups, especially those of the United States, striving for expansion and to reconquer for capitalism the socialist sector of the world. On the other hand, the Socialist States, whose advance depends on peace, together with the colonial peoples who have won their independence and those still struggling for liberation; and in the capitalist countries themselves (including the United States) the great majority of the people, who only suffer from war and from the economic and political consequences of war preparations.

Does the fact that imperialism drives to war mean that war is inevitable? Past experience seems to point to this conclusion. But to assume that this must also hold good in the future would be "dogmatic" Marxism, which takes no account of changed conditions, consideration of which is one of the most vital points in the Marxist approach. Today conditions have changed. The tendency to war is still there, and is obvious enough both in imperialist hostility to the Socialist countries and in the conflict of interests within the capitalist world itself as well as in colonial wars. But the new factors, briefly stated, are: the existence of a powerful socialist sector, also possessing nuclear weapons, so that war on it means mutual destruction; a world-wide movement of colonial liberation, so that it is not so easy today for imperialism to isolate and crush a single country, as was shown in the case of Egypt; and the strength of the opposition to war in the capitalist countries themselves, both in the working class movement and among the people generally. These new factors mean that war is today no longer inevitable, but can be prevented by the conscious action of the people, combined with the peace policy of the socialist countries and the liberated colonial countries – in the first place India. Peaceful co-existence, on the basis of mutual respect for each other's sovereignty, non-aggression and non-interference, equality and mutual advantage in all relations, and economic co-operation, is now possible.

The profound changes in the relation of class forces throughout the world also affect the problems of the transition to socialism in countries which are still capitalist.

Marx, in the conditions of his time, held that forcible revolution was the only way to displace the capitalist rulers and establish working class power to carry through the change to socialism. It is true that even at that time he excepted Britain and the United States; but this was on the ground that the military-bureaucratic State machine had not developed in these countries. Later, as Lenin pointed out in the First World War, this no longer applied. Experience has shown that Marx's insistence on the need for a forcible revolution was in fact justified in the case of Russia, where there were absolutely no possibilities of democratic change, because no democratic institutions existed. The experience was similar in China, although the way in which the revolution developed was different.

Today the further strengthening of the socialist sector of the world, and the weakening of the still existing capitalist system through the colonial liberation movement, have their counterpart in the growing strength of the working class and progressive movement in many capitalist countries. Although – especially in the United States – there are always tendencies towards the restriction of democratic rights, the working class and progressive movement is more and more determined to maintain and extend every aspect of democracy. Moreover, as monopoly capitalism, in its drive for ever higher profits, undermines the conditions of life of professional people and owners of small businesses, the resistance to reactionary policies becomes more widespread, and the way is opened for a broad alliance of the people for progressive aims. It is therefore now possible, especially in a country like Britain where there are long-established and highly developed democratic institutions and democratic tradition is strong, for the working class, if it is united and has the support of other progressive sections of the people, to use the historic institutions of their country, taking power from the capitalists and building Socialism. The essence is the taking of power; the form – forcible or peaceable – depends on the relative strength of the classes and the extent to which the capitalists themselves resort to force in the effort to turn back the wheel of history.

Thus Marxist theory, applied in new ways as conditions change, is able to guide the working class towards that line of action which, in the world conditions of today, will enable it most easily and rapidly to bring a socialist society into existence.

The historical stage in which the Russian workers achieved power, and the industrial, political and social backwardness of Tsarism which they had to overcome, made their task incredibly difficult. It was made even more difficult by foreign intervention: armed attacks from fourteen States in the early years; the terrible devastation of the Hitlerite invasion from 1941 to 1945. It was inevitable in such circumstances that force and compulsion would have to play an important part in safeguarding and building the new society, and that the people would have to pass through a long period of heavy sacrifices. But in spite of all difficulties, and in spite of the excesses of the later years of Stalin's regime, the Russian workers have built socialism in their country; and their victory has stimulated and inspired the tremendous revolutionary changes that have taken place throughout the world.

No country will have to pass through such experiences again in the advance of socialism. The very strength of the socialist sector of the world is now a bulwark against foreign intervention when the working people take power in another country. The vast industrial achievements of the Soviet Union are the basis on which the newer socialist countries are able to develop their own industry without such sacrifices as the Russian people had to make. The experience – positive and negative – of the Soviet transformation also makes the task easier for others.

Added to this is now the experience of People's China, which is of outstanding interest and importance for the transition to socialism in every country. Reference has already been made to the fact that conditions made possible the co-operation of capitalists in the transition, ending in the voluntary submergence of the great majority of capitalists in the new socialist organisation of production and distribution. This however is only one example of the approach that has been made, to all the problems of the transformation. Certainly, it was necessary to overthrow the Chiang regime by force, and it is still necessary to maintain forcible measures against Chiang's agents and other elements who resort to violence. But in the main, the principle is: "not forcibly, but by way of example, and by offering social aid" – which is the fundamental Marxist approach to the transformation of people. Education, persuasion, patience, respect for people – for their prejudices, and even for their status: these are some of the methods which countries advancing to socialism in the future will learn from the socialist countries.

New experience, too, will come increasingly from the former colonial countries which have won their independence. Their first problem is necessarily the building up of a modern industry, on which any substantial and general raising of the standard of living and culture must depend. It may well be that they will carry through this industrialisation – largely in the form of State-owned enterprises, thus in practice preparing the ground for the transition to socialism at no far distant date. In this development of industry they are being helped by the socialist countries, to which they are also drawn closer by the common interest in peace and resistance to aggressive imperialism.

The achievements of the socialist countries have had far-reaching consequences for the colonial peoples. In country after country they have thrown off foreign rule and are working to develop their countries for their own benefit. Even in those colonial territories which have not yet achieved their independence the wind of national liberation is rising to gale force.

The victory of the revolution in Cuba, the unity of its people in the struggle against the attacks organised by United States imperialism, and its rapid progress towards socialism with help of the socialist countries, have shown that Latin America is not outside this process.

The world is visibly in transition to Socialism: an immense area has already been withdrawn from capitalist and imperialist exploitation, and this area is growing, while the capitalist area is shrinking.

* * *

"Mankind," Marx said, "always only sets itself such problems as it can solve," for "the problem itself only arises when the material conditions for its solution are already present or at least in process of coming into being.''

Step by step, in its long struggle against the surrounding forces of Nature, mankind has raised itself above the brutes through human labour and skill, science and technique, until today it has reached the threshold of abundance and a good life for all. History now faces it with the problem of ending the class divisions in society which served human progress for some five thousand years but have now become a barrier to further advance. The material conditions for the solution of this problem are present today: the age of atomic energy and automation is the age of socialism.

Guided by the scientific theory of Marxism, a great part of mankind has already taken the leap into the next stage of human history. On the basis of their own experience and traditions the rest of mankind too will take this leap under the guidance of Marxism, bringing into being a truly human society throughout the world.